A VISUAL EXPLORATION OF SCIENCE

A VISUAL GUIDE TO
FISH AND AMPHIBIANS

Rosen
YA
New York

SOL90 EDITORIAL STAFF

This edition published in 2019 by:
The Rosen Publishing Group, Inc.
29 East 21st Street
New York, NY 10010

Cataloging-in-Publication Data

Names: Editorial Sol90 (Firm).
Title: A visual guide to fish and amphibians / edited by the Sol90 Editorial Staff.
Description: New York : Rosen YA, 2019. | Series: A visual exploration of science | Includes glossary and index.
Identifiers: LCCN ISBN 9781508182344 (pbk.) | ISBN 9781508182337 (library bound)
Subjects: LCSH: Fishes–Juvenile literature. | Amphibians–Juvenile literature.
Classification: LCC QL617.2 V578 2019 | DDC 597–dc23

Manufactured in the United States of America

Project Management: Nuria Cicero
Editorial Coordination: Alberto Hernández, Joan Soriano, Diana Malizia
Proofreaders: Marta Kordon, Edgardo D'Elio
Layout: Laura Ocampo

Photo Credits: Age Fotostock, Getty Images, Science Photo Library, Graphic News, ESA, NASA, National Geographic, Latinstock, Album, ACI, Cordon Press, Shutterstock

Illustrators: Guido Arroyo, Pablo Aschei, Gustavo J. Caironi, Hernán Cañellas, Leonardo César, José Luis Corsetti, Vanina Farías, Manrique Fernández Buente, Joana Garrido, Celina Hilbert, Jorge Ivanovich, Isidro López, Diego Martín, Jorge Martínez, Marco Menco, Marcelo Morán, Ala de Mosca, Diego Mourelos, Eduardo Pérez, Javier Pérez, Ariel Piroyansky, Fernando Ramallo, Ariel Roldán, Marcel Socías, Néstor Taylor, Trebol Animation, Juan Venegas, Constanza Vicco, Coralia Vignau, Gustavo Yamin, 3DN, 3DOM studio.

Contents

Water, the Source of Life

he life of marine creatures is fascinating and has always been closely linked to human life. This is because fishing has been the livelihood of islanders through the years. Yet for some time, in many areas of the world—such as Nha Trang Bay, on the south coast of Vietnam—this activity has been in a state of crisis. In Nha Trang Bay the growth of

outside investment in aquaculture has limited the economic opportunities of the local population, including fishing for squid and other species in the reefs with hook and line. In other cases, commercial fishing endangers the future of those who rely on traditional fishing methods to make a living. This is only one of the topics explored in this book, which also relates in detail many secrets of these vertebrates, which were among the first creatures with skeletons to appear on the Earth. Perhaps knowing more about their habits and modes of life may move us to care for them and protect them. They are at the mercy of variations in water conditions to a greater extent than humans.

Humans have marveled for centuries at the fact that, after journeying across the ocean, salmon can find the river where they were born. Is this navigational ability related to the Earth's magnetic field, sense of smell, instinct, or something else that humans cannot even imagine? For those interested in statistics, in the Yukon River in Alaska and in Canada, certain tagged Chinook salmon covered nearly 2,000 miles (3,200 km) in 60 days. Upon entering the river, the salmon stop eating and utilize the fat they accumulated while in the ocean. After laying their eggs, many of the females die. Most ocean fish seek shallow, nutrient-rich waters in which to lay their eggs. That is why coastal waters and estuaries are so important to the life cycle of many species. Another oddity of these animals is that they have adapted to living in a variety of aquatic habitats: rivers, lakes, estuaries, coral reefs,

and the open sea. For this reason, they have developed various survival techniques to live in such a wide variety of places.

Despite the fact that lunglike sacs evolved because of the difficulty of breathing with gills in water with low oxygen content, the development of these sacs was also the first step toward moving onto land. Some descendants of the first fish with fleshy, jointed fins, known as lobe-fin fishes, began to find terrestrial food sources and, with time, adapted more completely to life on the planet's surface. This evolutionary change—passing from an aquatic to a terrestrial medium—constituted a true revolution for the life-forms that existed up until then. The amphibians we will show you in this book that are living today are a tiny representation of all those that appeared during the Devonian Period, most of which became extinct during the Triassic Period.

Amphibians, especially some frog species, have become true specialists in the art of mimicry. One of the most fascinating examples is the European tree frog, which changes color to regulate its body temperature. On warm, dry evenings the frog rests in sunny places, and its skin is pale. As its surroundings become cooler, the frog darkens to absorb heat. Although amphibians are masters of camouflage, which protects them from predators, at present they are the object of worldwide concern because of the dramatic decline in their populations. Turn the page, and you will discover much more about the abilities of fish and amphibians, extraordinary creatures that live right next to us.

General Characteristics

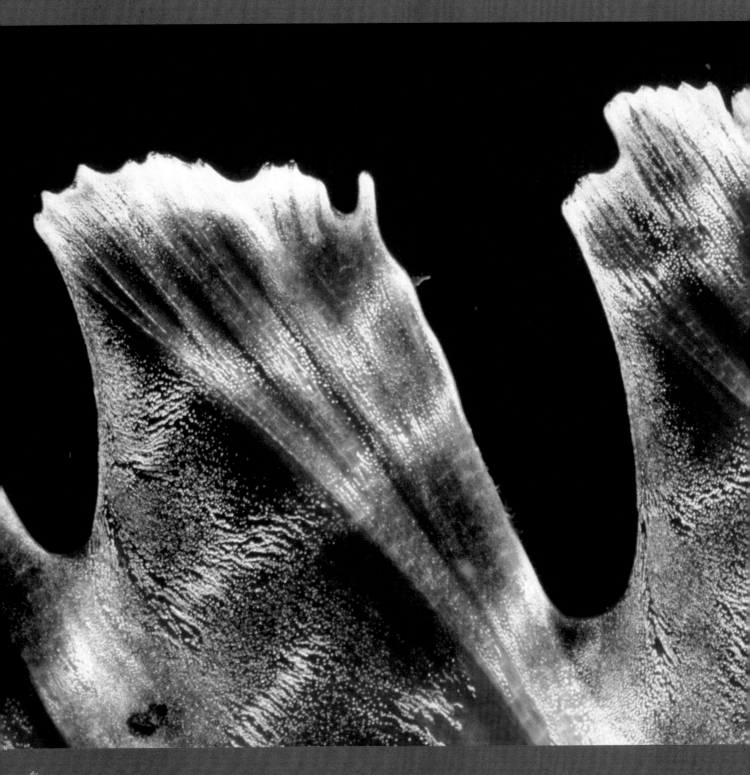

Fish were the first vertebrates with bony skeletons to appear on the Earth. They doubtless form the most numerous group of vertebrates. Unlike today's fish, the earliest fish had no scales, fins, or jawbone, but they did have a type of dorsal fin. Over time they have been changing in form and size to adapt to different environments, in both fresh

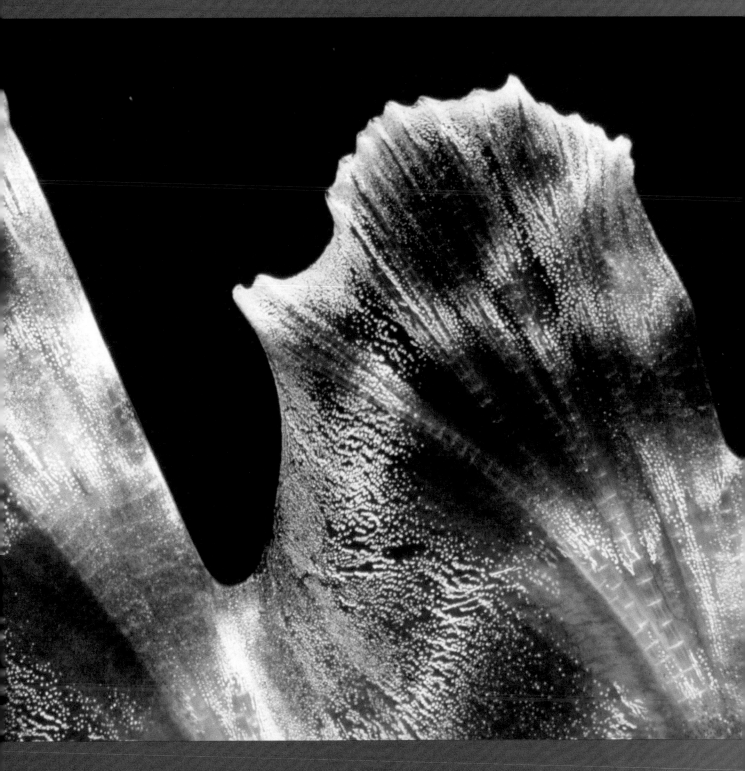

water and salt water. Their bodies are generally streamlined and covered with smooth scales. They have fins that enable them to move with energy, direction, and stability. In place of lungs, these complex creatures normally breathe through gills that capture oxygen dissolved in the water, and they are cold blooded. ●

Earliest Forms

About 470 million years ago, the first fish appeared. Unlike today's fish, they did not have a jawbone, fins, or scales. Hard plates covered the front part of the fish and formed a protective shield. They also had a solid, flexible dorsal spine that allowed them to propel themselves. Later, in the Silurian Period, fish appeared that had a jawbone. Known as the gnathostomata, they were large predators. ●

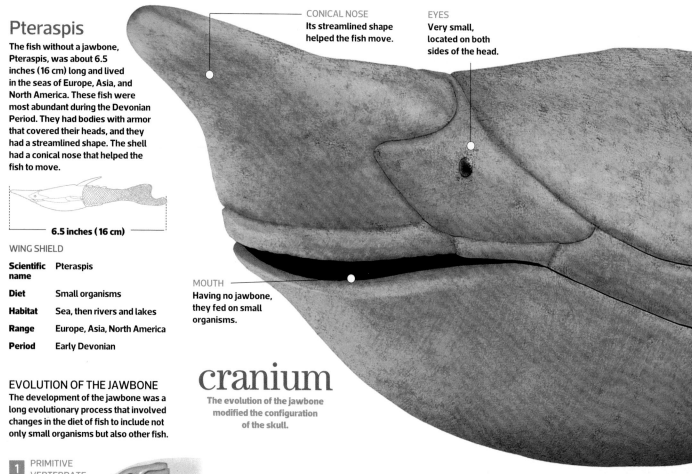

Pteraspis

The fish without a jawbone, Pteraspis, was about 6.5 inches (16 cm) long and lived in the seas of Europe, Asia, and North America. These fish were most abundant during the Devonian Period. They had bodies with armor that covered their heads, and they had a streamlined shape. The shell had a conical nose that helped the fish to move.

6.5 inches (16 cm)

WING SHIELD

Scientific name	Pteraspis
Diet	Small organisms
Habitat	Sea, then rivers and lakes
Range	Europe, Asia, North America
Period	Early Devonian

CONICAL NOSE
Its streamlined shape helped the fish move.

EYES
Very small, located on both sides of the head.

MOUTH
Having no jawbone, they fed on small organisms.

cranium
The evolution of the jawbone modified the configuration of the skull.

EVOLUTION OF THE JAWBONE
The development of the jawbone was a long evolutionary process that involved changes in the diet of fish to include not only small organisms but also other fish.

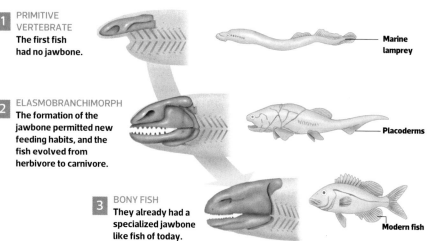

1 PRIMITIVE VERTEBRATE
The first fish had no jawbone.

2 ELASMOBRANCHIMORPH
The formation of the jawbone permitted new feeding habits, and the fish evolved from herbivore to carnivore.

3 BONY FISH
They already had a specialized jawbone like fish of today.

Marine lamprey

Placoderms

Modern fish

Fossil

◤◢ Fish with lungs appeared in the Mesozoic Era (200 million years ago). Similar to amphibians, these species breathe with lungs and are now considered living fossils. The line through the center of the photo of the fossil is the fish's lateral line.

FOSSILIZED LUNGFISH SCALES
Dipterus valenciennesi

Dunkleosteus

The Arthrodira—with a jointed neck—were armored fish that predominated in the late Devonian Period. The Devonian predator Dunkleosteus was an arthrodiran placoderm that lived over 300 million years ago. Its head was encased in an impressive set of plates 1.2 inches (cm) thick, with razor-sharp bony plates that served as teeth.

STREAMLINED SHAPE
The shape of Pteraspis shows that it was an excellent swimmer.

FIERCE JAW
Dunkleosteus was a fierce predator that devoured any type of prey, including sharks.

DORSAL SPIKE
Located on the fish's back, it worked like a dorsal fin.

DORSAL SPINES
These helped the fish to stay balanced while swimming.

LATERAL LINE
Sensory organs are present on both sides of the body and on top of the armor.

Its head was protected by strong armor.

Dorsal fin

The tail was not protected by scales.

This area of the body had neither armor nor scales.

It had a lobed tail, similar to a shark's tail, which indicates that it was a powerful swimmer.

It also had strong jaws with bony teeth.

16 feet (5 m)
LENGTH OF THE FISH

TAIL
The shape of the tail helped balance the weight of the armor.

Evolution

In the Devonian Period ocean fish began to diversify. Coelacanths appeared, as well as the earliest bony fish and the first cartilaginous fish, including sharks. In this period the three main groups of gnathostomad fish also appeared: the placoderms, chondrichthyes, and osteichthyes.

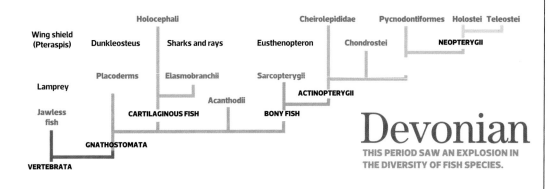

Chimaeriformes　　　　Cheirolepis　　Pycnodus　　Sole

Holocephali　　　　　　Cheirolepididae　　Pycnodontiformes　Holostei　Teleostei

Wing shield (Pteraspis)　Dunkleosteus　　Sharks and rays　　Eusthenopteron　Chondrostei　NEOPTERYGII

Lamprey　　Placoderms　　Elasmobranchii　　Sarcopterygii　ACTINOPTERYGII

Jawless fish　　　　　　Acanthodii

CARTILAGINOUS FISH　　　BONY FISH

GNATHOSTOMATA

VERTEBRATA

Devonian
THIS PERIOD SAW AN EXPLOSION IN THE DIVERSITY OF FISH SPECIES.

Distinguishing Features

S imilar characteristics define nearly all fish, with a few rare exceptions. These aquatic animals are designed to live underwater, and they have a jawbone and lidless eyes and are cold blooded. They breathe through gills and are vertebrates—that is, they have a spinal column. They live in the oceans, from the poles to the equator, as well as in bodies of fresh water and in streams. Some fish migrate, but very few can pass from salt water to fresh water or vice versa. Their fins enable them to swim and move in different directions. Animals such as dolphins, seals, and whales are at times mistaken for fish, but they are actually mammals. ●

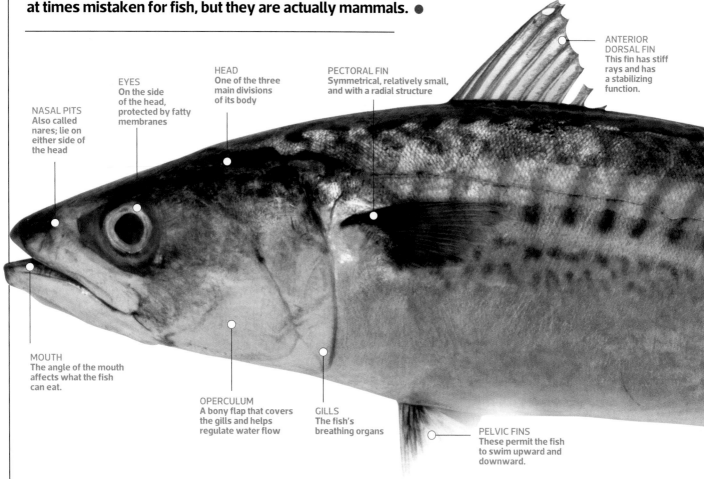

NASAL PITS
Also called nares; lie on either side of the head

EYES
On the side of the head, protected by fatty membranes

HEAD
One of the three main divisions of its body

PECTORAL FIN
Symmetrical, relatively small, and with a radial structure

ANTERIOR DORSAL FIN
This fin has stiff rays and has a stabilizing function.

MOUTH
The angle of the mouth affects what the fish can eat.

OPERCULUM
A bony flap that covers the gills and helps regulate water flow

GILLS
The fish's breathing organs

PELVIC FINS
These permit the fish to swim upward and downward.

Gill Breathing

Gills are the organs that fish use to breathe. They are made of filaments linked by the gill arches. The fish uses its gills to take in oxygen dissolved in the water. Through a process known as diffusion, oxygen is transferred to the blood, which has a lower concentration of oxygen than the water. In this way the fish oxygenates its blood, which then circulates to the rest of its body. In most bony fish (osteichthyes) water flows in through the mouth, splits into two streams, and exits through the gill slits.

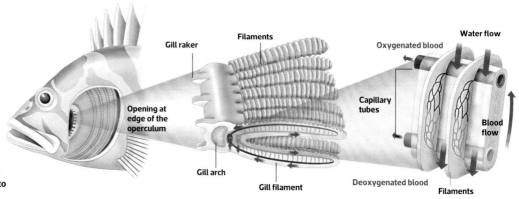

Gill raker

Filaments

Water flow

Oxygenated blood

Opening at edge of the operculum

Capillary tubes

Blood flow

Gill arch

Gill filament

Deoxygenated blood

Filaments

Near-fossils

Choanichthyes (Sarcopterygii) are archaic bony fish with fleshy fins. Some of them were the first animals with lungs. Only a few species survive.

Jawless Fish

Of the ancient agnathans, considered the first living vertebrates, only lampreys and hagfish are left.

SEA LAMPREY *Lampetra* sp.
Its round, toothed mouth allows it to suck the blood of fish of various species. There are also freshwater lampreys.

COELACANTH *Latimeria chalumnae*
This species was thought to have gone extinct millions of years ago, until one was discovered alive off the coast of South Africa in 1938; more of these fish were found later.

SCALES
The scales are lubricated, meaning they overlap one another.

POSTERIOR DORSAL FIN
This soft-structured fin is located between the dorsal fin and the tail.

Just Cartilage

Cartilaginous fish, such as rays and sharks, have extremely flexible skeletons with little or no bone.

RAY *Raja miraletus*
Its large fins send currents of water carrying plankton and small fish to its mouth. The ray is very fast.

LATERAL LINE
Fish have sensory organs all along this line.

With Spines

Osteichthyes is the most numerous class of fish. The skeleton has some level of calcification.

ATLANTIC MACKEREL *Scomber scombrus*
This fish has no teeth. It lives in temperate waters, and its meat is considered delicious. It can live for more than 10 years.

ANAL FIN
Soft, with a row of finlets

TAIL MUSCLE
This is the strongest muscle in the fish.

CAUDAL FIN
It moves from side to side, propelling the fish forward.

In Action
Water enters the mouth and flows over the gills. After the gills extract oxygen, the water is expelled through the gill slits.

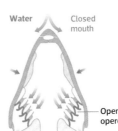

Water | Open mouth
Pharynx
Gills
Closed operculum
Esophagus

Water | Closed mouth
Open operculum

Operculum
Opens and closes the openings where water exits

25,000
Is the number of known fish species, making up nearly one half of all chordate species.

Bony Fish

The group of fish that have evolved and diversified most in the last few million years are the osteichthyes, fish with spines and jawbones. In general, their skeletons are relatively small but firm, being made mostly of bone. Flexible fins enable them to control their movements with precision. The various species of osteichthyes have adapted to a wide variety of environments and even to extreme conditions. ●

Solid Structure

➤ The skeleton of a bony fish is divided into the cranium, spinal column, and fins. The opercula, which cover their gills, are also made of bone. The cranium holds the brain and supports the jawbone and gill arches. The vertebrae of the spine are jointed; they provide support to the body and join the ribs at the abdomen.

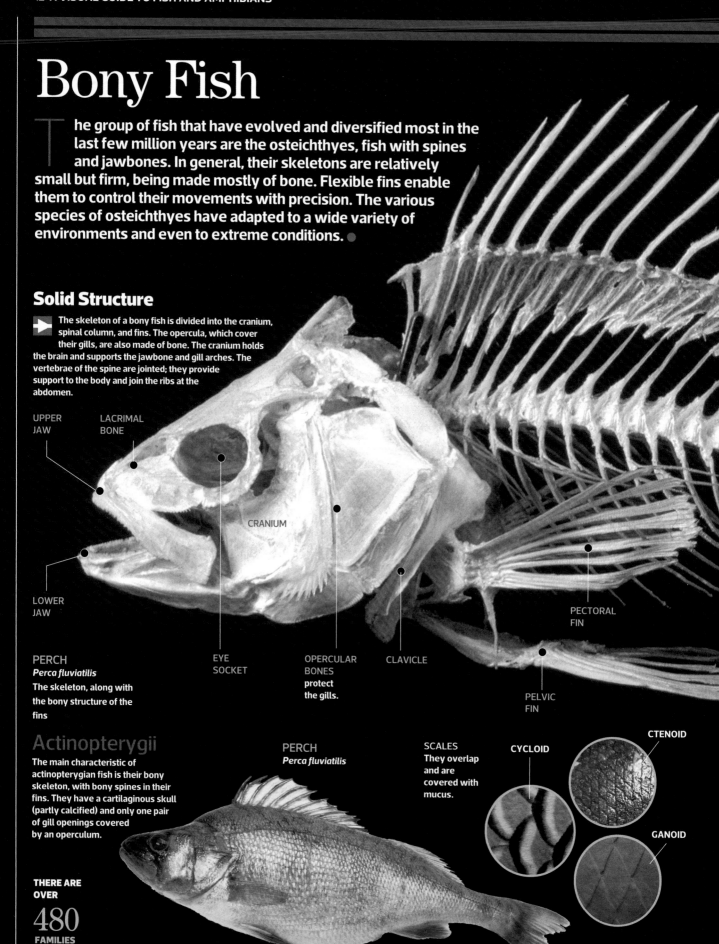

UPPER JAW

LACRIMAL BONE

CRANIUM

LOWER JAW

PECTORAL FIN

EYE SOCKET

OPERCULAR BONES
protect the gills.

CLAVICLE

PELVIC FIN

PERCH
Perca fluviatilis
The skeleton, along with the bony structure of the fins

Actinopterygii

The main characteristic of actinopterygian fish is their bony skeleton, with bony spines in their fins. They have a cartilaginous skull (partly calcified) and only one pair of gill openings covered by an operculum.

PERCH
Perca fluviatilis

SCALES
They overlap and are covered with mucus.

CYCLOID

CTENOID

GANOID

THERE ARE OVER

480
FAMILIES

OCEAN SUNFISH
Mola mola
The largest osteichthian fish, it can grow to be 11 feet (3.3 m) long and can weigh 4,000 pounds (1,900 kg).

The Swim Bladder

An appendage of the intestines that regulates flotation by filling with and emptying itself of gas. The gas enters through a gland that extracts the gas from a net of capillaries, called the rete mirabile, and it leaves the bladder through a valve that causes it to dissolve back into the blood.

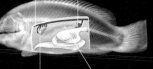

EMPTY
When the fish empties its swim bladder, it sinks.

FULL
By reducing its density, the fish rises.

Rete Mirabile   Dorsal Aorta

Gas Gland   SWIM BLADDER

FIRST DORSAL FIN

SECOND DORSAL FIN

VERTEBRA
- Neural spine
- Neural arch
- Centrum
- Hemal arch (chevron)
- Hemal spine

VERTEBRAL COLUMN
The main nerves and blood vessels run above and below the bony center of the spine.

CAUDAL FIN VERTEBRAE

RIB

SPINY RAYS OF ANAL FIN

INTERHEMAL (VENTRAL) SPINES
support the spiny rays of the anal fin.

CAUDAL FIN
propels the fish through the water.

Sarcopterygii

Another name for the Choanichthyes, a subclass of bony fish. Their fins, like the fins of whales, are joined to the body by means of fleshy lobes. In lungfish, these lobed fins look like filaments.

COELACANTH
Latimeria chalumnae

DETAIL OF FLESHY FIN

Cartilaginous Fish

As indicated by the name, the skeleton of cartilaginous fish is made of cartilage, a flexible, durable substance that is softer than bone. They have jaws and teeth, which are usually hard and sharp. Their body is covered with hard scales. However, they lack a characteristic shared by most bony fish—the swim bladder, an organ that helps fish to float. Their pectoral fins, tail, and flat head give this group a streamlined profile.

Sharks

These fish live in tropical waters, although some do inhabit temperate waters or fresh water. They have an elongated, cylindrical shape and a pointed snout, with the mouth on the underside. Each side of their head has five to seven gill slits.

BLOOD
They are cold blooded.

2,650 pounds
(1.2 metric tons)
NORMAL WEIGHT OF A SHARK
(*SUPERORDER SELACHIMORPHA*)

LIGHT AND FLEXIBLE
The skeleton is very flexible, but the spinal column of cartilage is firm, with mineral deposits.

SPINAL COLUMN

Nostril

SHARP TEETH
The teeth are triangular in shape. All chondrichthyes lose their teeth and grow new ones.

Surface pore

Epidermis

Sensory cells

Nerves

Gelatinous tract

Heat-generating muscles

ACUTE SENSES
Chondrichthyes have ampullae of Lorenzini, acutely sensitive lateral lines, and a highly developed sense of smell.

AMPULLAE OF LORENZINI
detect electric signals transmitted by potential prey.

GILL SLITS
These life-forms may have five or six gill slits.

Primitive

The ancient origin of Chondrichthyes contrasts sharply with their highly evolved senses. This is a fossilized cartilage vertebra of a shark from the Paleozoic Era, between 245 and 540 million years ago. It was found in a fossil deposit in Kent, England. The blood of sharks has a high concentration of urea, which is presumed to be an adaptation to salt water and constitutes a fundamental difference between sharks and their freshwater ancestors.

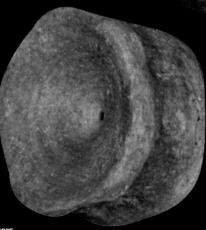

Manta Rays and Skates

These fish have two pectoral fins joined on the front of the body. They use them to swim, giving the impression that they fly in the water. The rest of the body moves similarly to a whip. Their eyes are located on the upper side of the body; the mouth and gills are on the lower side.

RAY
Raja clavata (Thornback Ray)
This species lives in cold oceans in depths up to 660 feet (200 m).

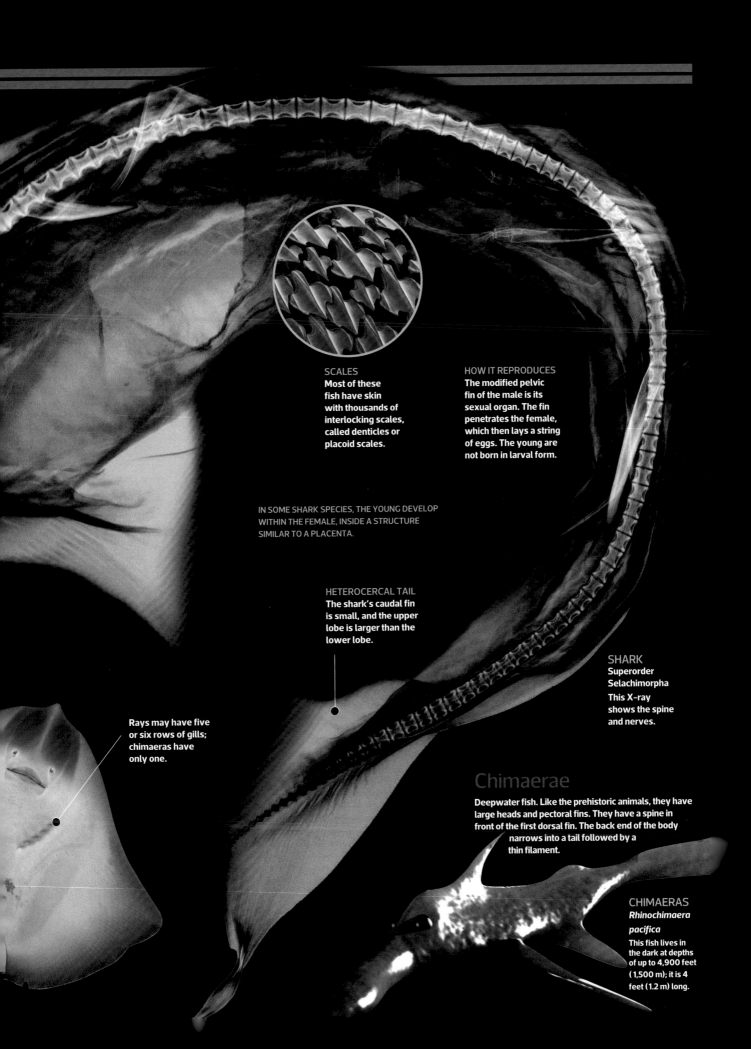

SCALES
Most of these fish have skin with thousands of interlocking scales, called denticles or placoid scales.

HOW IT REPRODUCES
The modified pelvic fin of the male is its sexual organ. The fin penetrates the female, which then lays a string of eggs. The young are not born in larval form.

IN SOME SHARK SPECIES, THE YOUNG DEVELOP WITHIN THE FEMALE, INSIDE A STRUCTURE SIMILAR TO A PLACENTA.

HETEROCERCAL TAIL
The shark's caudal fin is small, and the upper lobe is larger than the lower lobe.

SHARK
Superorder Selachimorpha
This X-ray shows the spine and nerves.

Rays may have five or six rows of gills; chimaeras have only one.

Chimaerae

Deepwater fish. Like the prehistoric animals, they have large heads and pectoral fins. They have a spine in front of the first dorsal fin. The back end of the body narrows into a tail followed by a thin filament.

CHIMAERAS
Rhinochimaera pacifica
This fish lives in the dark at depths of up to 4,900 feet (1,500 m); it is 4 feet (1.2 m) long.

Anatomy

M ost fish have the same internal organs as amphibians, reptiles, birds, and mammals. The skeleton acts as a support, and the brain receives information through the eyes and the lateral line to coordinate the motions of the muscles in propelling the fish through the water. Fish breathe with gills, they have a digestive system designed to transform food into nutrients, and they have a heart that pumps blood through a network of blood vessels. ●

SIMPLE EYE
Each eye focuses to one side; there is no binocular vision.

BRAIN
receives information and coordinates all the fish's actions and functions.

Suspensory ligament
Lens
Iris
Retina
Optic nerve

MOUTH

GILLS
Structures with multiple folds that provide oxygen to the blood

HEART
receives all the blood and pumps it toward the gills.

LIVER

Cyclostomata

Its digestive tract is little more than a straight tube extending from its round, jawless mouth to the anus. Because of their simplicity, many species of lampreys are parasites. They live off the blood of other fish and have thin pharyngeal sacs instead of gills.

45 THE CURRENT NUMBER OF SPECIES OF CYCLOSTOMATA

CAUDAL FIN

ANUS

EYE

BREATHING SACS

HEART

LIVER

TOOTHED MOUTH

FIRST DORSAL FIN

LAMPREY
Lampetra sp.

INTESTINE

SUPPORT FOR PHARYNGEAL SACS

NOTOCHORD

TESTICLES

VERTEBRAE

STOMACH

BRAIN

RIGHT KIDNEY

GONAD

Chondrichthyes

A shark has the same organic structures as a bony fish, except for the swim bladder. A shark also has a corkscrew-like structure called a spiral valve at the end of its intestine to increase the surface area for absorption of nutrients.

NASAL PIT

SHARK
Carcharodon sp.

MOUTH

GILL SLITS

HEART

LIVER

STOMACH

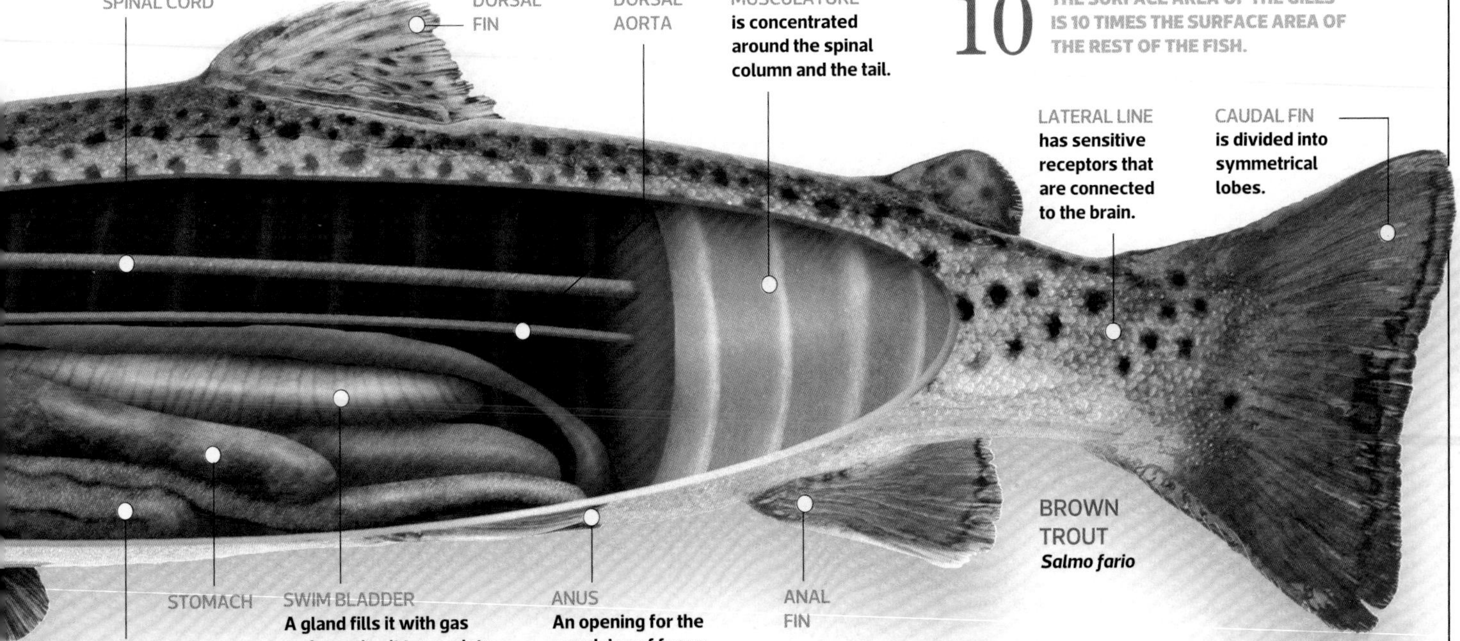

10 THE SURFACE AREA OF THE GILLS IS 10 TIMES THE SURFACE AREA OF THE REST OF THE FISH.

Osteichthyes

Typically, their organs are compressed in the lower front quarter of the body. The rest of their internal structure consists mainly of the muscles that the fish uses to swim. Some bony fish, such as carp, have no stomach but rather a tightly coiled intestine.

REGULATION OF SALINITY

FRESHWATER FISH

Freshwater fish run the risk of losing salt to their environment. They drink only a small quantity of water, and they obtain additional salt from their food.

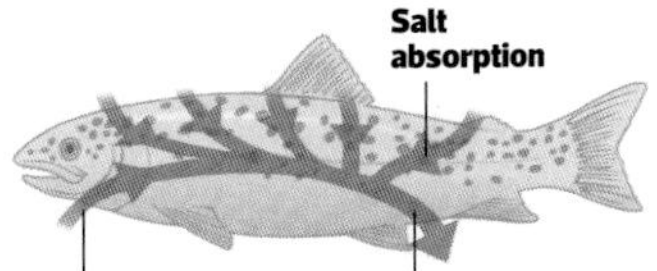

SALTWATER FISH

These fish constantly absorb salt water to replenish the water in their bodies, but they must eliminate excess salt from the marine environment.

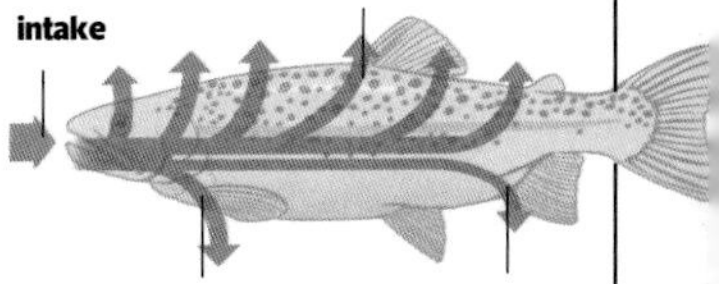

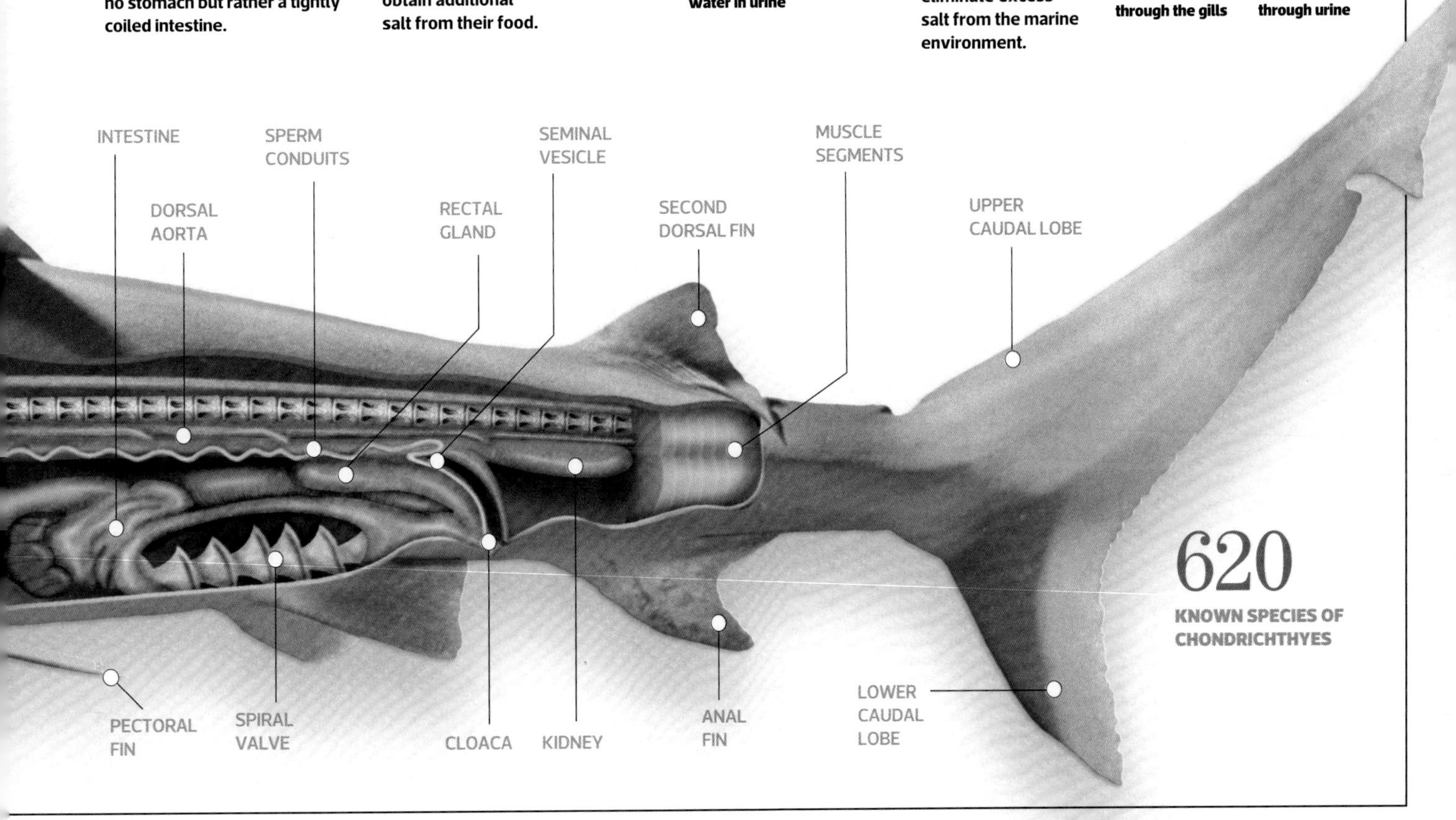

620 KNOWN SPECIES OF CHONDRICHTHYES

Life in the Water

The idea that fish are blind is wrong. Most fish have the best possible eyesight for their habitat. Further, they can see in color and use colors to camouflage themselves or defend their territory. Most fish can vary their coloring when something changes in their environment. Silverfish, common in all freshwater habitats, have dark

GLOBEFISH
When threatened, this strange animal reacts by swallowing water until it blows up like a balloon.

backs (ranging from greenish brown to dark blue), but the sides of their bellies are silvery white. When viewed from above, their backs become confused with the deep hues of the river water or even with the crystalline blue of lakes. Seen from below, the lower part becomes confused with bright reflections in the water. ●

Protective Layer

M ost fish are covered with scales, an external layer of transparent plates. All fish of a given species have the same number of scales. Depending on the family and genus of a fish, its scales can have a variety of characteristics. Scales on the lateral line of the body have small orifices that link the surface with a series of sensory cells and nerve endings. It is also possible to determine a fish's age by studying its scales. ●

FOSSILIZED SCALES

The remains of these thick, shiny, enameled scales belong to the extinct genus *Lepidotes*, a fish that lived during the Mesozoic Era.

External focus

Internal radius

SCALE REGENERATION

Scales grow back after a lesion, but the new ones are different from the original scales.

Original scales

Rhomboid shield

Internal filament

Protuberance

Base

EDGES
are overlapping, with a smooth texture.

TOOTHED SCALE
With enamel

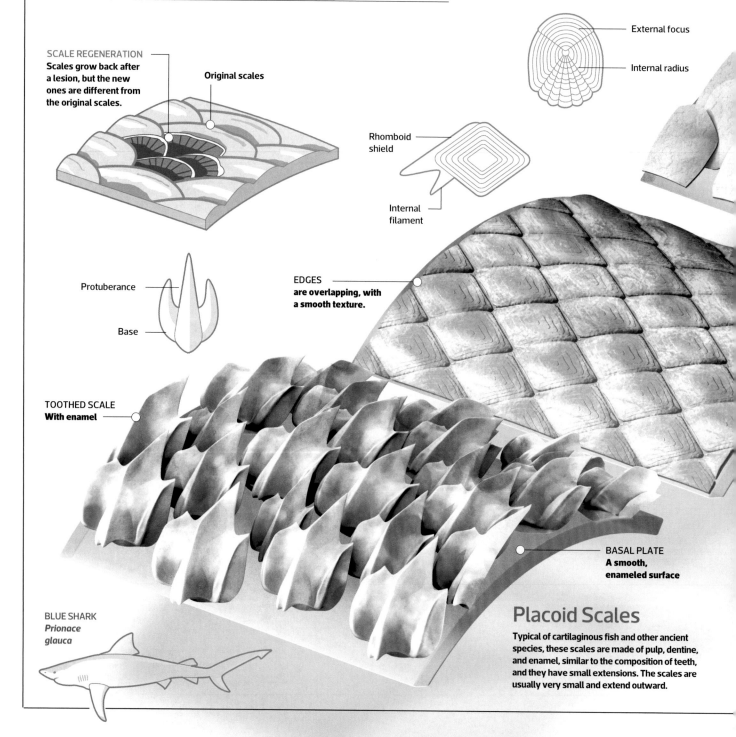

BASAL PLATE
A smooth, enameled surface

BLUE SHARK
Prionace glauca

Placoid Scales

Typical of cartilaginous fish and other ancient species, these scales are made of pulp, dentine, and enamel, similar to the composition of teeth, and they have small extensions. The scales are usually very small and extend outward.

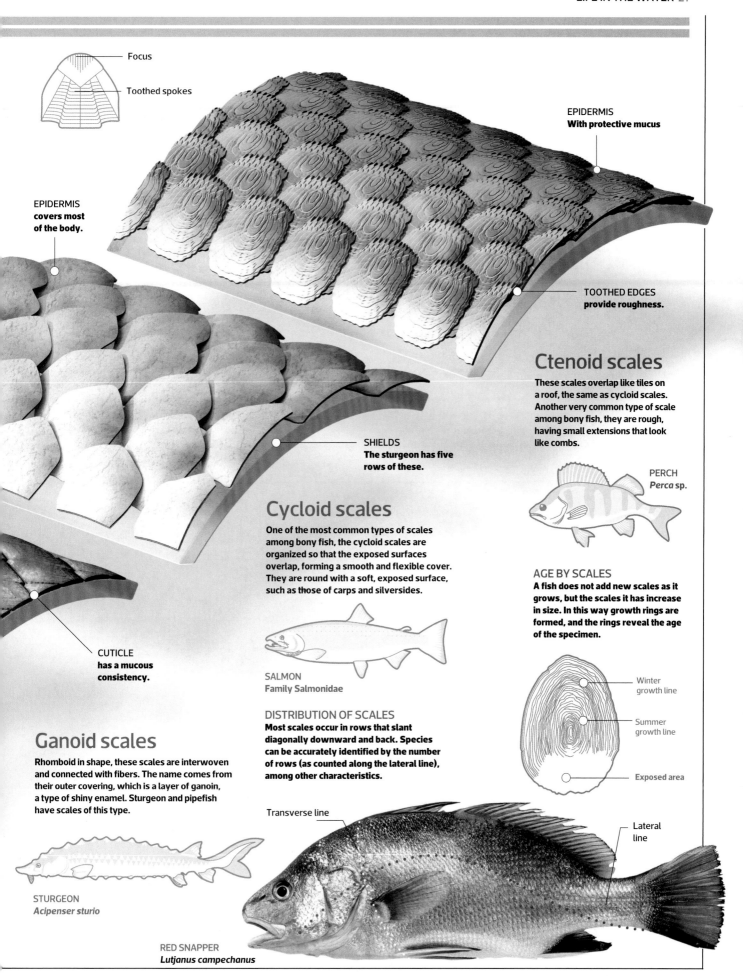

Focus

Toothed spokes

EPIDERMIS
With protective mucus

EPIDERMIS
**covers most
of the body.**

TOOTHED EDGES
provide roughness.

Ctenoid scales

**These scales overlap like tiles on
a roof, the same as cycloid scales.
Another very common type of scale
among bony fish, they are rough,
having small extensions that look
like combs.**

SHIELDS
**The sturgeon has five
rows of these.**

PERCH
Perca sp.

Cycloid scales

**One of the most common types of scales
among bony fish, the cycloid scales are
organized so that the exposed surfaces
overlap, forming a smooth and flexible cover.
They are round with a soft, exposed surface,
such as those of carps and silversides.**

AGE BY SCALES
**A fish does not add new scales as it
grows, but the scales it has increase
in size. In this way growth rings are
formed, and the rings reveal the age
of the specimen.**

CUTICLE
**has a mucous
consistency.**

SALMON
Family Salmonidae

Winter
growth line

Summer
growth line

DISTRIBUTION OF SCALES
**Most scales occur in rows that slant
diagonally downward and back. Species
can be accurately identified by the number
of rows (as counted along the lateral line),
among other characteristics.**

Exposed area

Ganoid scales

**Rhomboid in shape, these scales are interwoven
and connected with fibers. The name comes from
their outer covering, which is a layer of ganoin,
a type of shiny enamel. Sturgeon and pipefish
have scales of this type.**

Transverse line

Lateral
line

STURGEON
Acipenser sturio

RED SNAPPER
Lutjanus campechanus

Extremities

A fish can control its motion, direction, and stability by means of its fins and tail. Anatomically these are extensions of the skin beyond the body and, in most bony fish, are supported by rays. The fins reveal much about the life of each fish. Thin fins with a split tail indicate that the animal moves very quickly, or it may need them to cover great distances. On the other hand, fish that live among rocks and reefs near the ocean floor have broad lateral fins and large tails. ●

GOLDFISH
Carassius auratus
A species bred for its beauty. Its tail can have eight different shapes.

SIAMESE FIGHTING FISH
Betta splendens
spreads its fins like a fan when it jumps.

FIN RAYS
Bony filaments that are joined by a membrane

The highest and longest lobe turns upward.

GREY REEF SHARK
Carcharhinus amblyrhynchos
The heterocercal tail is typical of these cartilaginous fish, as well as of sturgeons.

The spinal column ends in a broadened structure.

Homocercal Tail

The caudal fin is divided into two equal lobes, an upper and a lower lobe, which extend from the end of the spinal column.

1/8 The proportion of the length of a salmon's homocercal tail with respect to its body.

The Typical Tail

The vast majority of bony fish have homocercal tails.

Heterocercal Tail

Its two lobes are uneven. The dorsal spine turns upward in the highest lobe, and the rays that form the two lobes of the caudal fin extend from the lower end of the spinal column.

The shark's spine extends into the upper lobe of the caudal fin.

1/3 The proportion of the lower lobe of the tail to the upper lobe of the tail

The lower lobe is smaller and is merely a projection to the side of the spine.

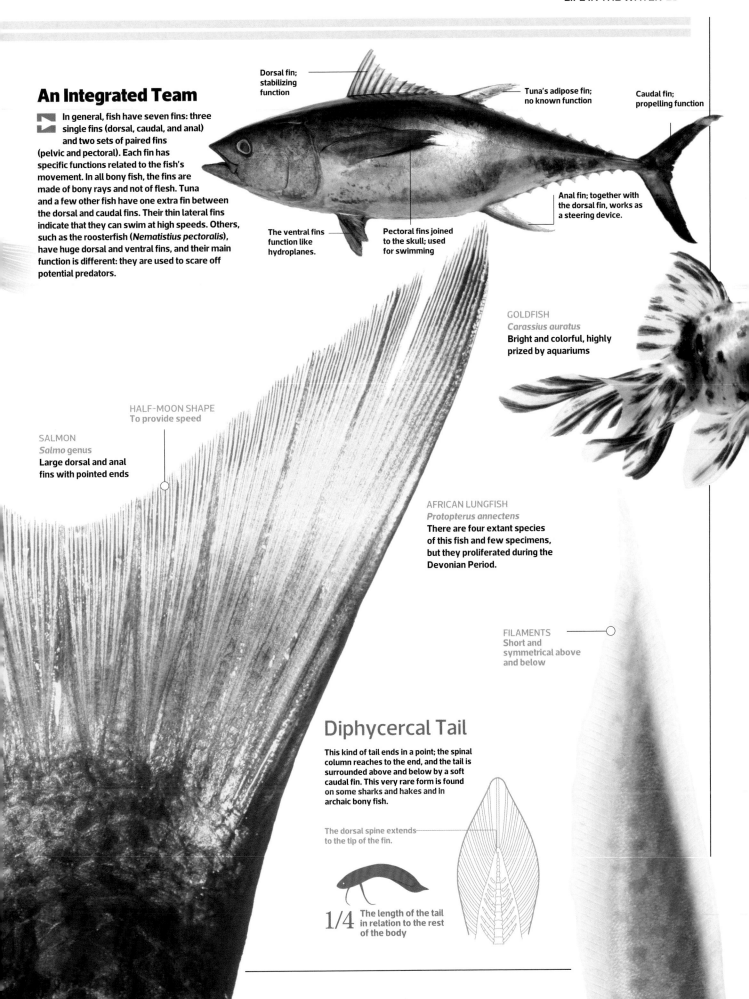

An Integrated Team

In general, fish have seven fins: three single fins (dorsal, caudal, and anal) and two sets of paired fins (pelvic and pectoral). Each fin has specific functions related to the fish's movement. In all bony fish, the fins are made of bony rays and not of flesh. Tuna and a few other fish have one extra fin between the dorsal and caudal fins. Their thin lateral fins indicate that they can swim at high speeds. Others, such as the roosterfish (*Nematistius pectoralis*), have huge dorsal and ventral fins, and their main function is different: they are used to scare off potential predators.

Dorsal fin; stabilizing function

Tuna's adipose fin; no known function

Caudal fin; propelling function

Anal fin; together with the dorsal fin, works as a steering device.

The ventral fins function like hydroplanes.

Pectoral fins joined to the skull; used for swimming

GOLDFISH
Carassius auratus
Bright and colorful, highly prized by aquariums

HALF-MOON SHAPE
To provide speed

SALMON
Salmo genus
Large dorsal and anal fins with pointed ends

AFRICAN LUNGFISH
Protopterus annectens
There are four extant species of this fish and few specimens, but they proliferated during the Devonian Period.

FILAMENTS
Short and symmetrical above and below

Diphycercal Tail

This kind of tail ends in a point; the spinal column reaches to the end, and the tail is surrounded above and below by a soft caudal fin. This very rare form is found on some sharks and hakes and in archaic bony fish.

The dorsal spine extends to the tip of the fin.

1/4 The length of the tail in relation to the rest of the body

The Art of Swimming

To swim, fish move in three dimensions: forward and back, left and right, and up and down. The main control surfaces that fish use for maneuvering are the fins, including the tail, or caudal fin. To change direction, the fish tilts the control surfaces at an angle to the water current. The fish must also keep its balance in the water; it accomplishes this by moving its paired and unpaired fins. ●

UPSIDE-DOWN CATFISH
Synodontis nigriventris

This fish swims upside down, seeking food sources that are less accessible to other species.

MUSCLES
The tail has powerful muscles that enable it to move like an oar.

GREAT WHITE SHARK
Carcharodon carcharias

Red muscles are for slow or regular movements.

Larger white muscles are for moving with speed, but they tire easily.

Starting Out
The movement of a fish through the water is like that of a slithering snake. Its body goes through a series of wavelike movements similar to an S curve. This process begins when the fish moves its head slightly from side to side.

The crest of the body's wave moves from back to front.

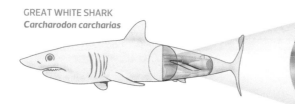

In its side-to-side movement, the tail displaces the water.

At first the tail is even with the head.

STREAMLINED SHAPE
Like the keel of a ship, the rounded contours of a fish are instrumental. In addition, most of a fish's volume is in the front part of its body. As the fish swims forward, its shape causes the density of the water ahead to be reduced relative to the density of the water behind. This reduces the water's resistance.

The head moves from side to side.

THE FISH'S KEEL
A ship has a heavy keel in the lower part to keep it from capsizing. Fish, on the other hand, have the keel on top. If the paired fins stop functioning to keep the fish balanced, the fish turns over because its heaviest part tends to sink, which happens when fish die.

KEEL   LIVE FISH   DEAD FISH

THE FASTEST

The powerful caudal fin displaces large amounts of water.

SAILFISH
Istiophorus platypterus

The unfurled dorsal fin can be up to 150 percent of the width of the fish's body.

Its long upper jaw enables it to slice through the water, aiding this fish's hydrodynamics.

70 miles per hour (109 km/h)
The maximum swimming speed it attains

Forward Motion

results from the synchronized S-curve movement of the muscles surrounding the spinal column. These muscles usually make alternating lateral motions. Fish with large pectoral fins use them like oars for propulsion.

The oarlike movement of the tail is the main force used for forward motion.

The dorsal fin **keeps the fish upright.**

The pectoral fins **maintain balance and can act as brakes.**

The ventral fins **stabilize the fish for proper balance.**

Balance

When the fish is moving slowly or is still in the water, the fins can be seen making small movements to keep the body in balance.

Upward and Downward

The angle of the fins relative to the body allows the fish to move up or down. The paired fins, located in front of the center of gravity, are used for this upward or downward movement.

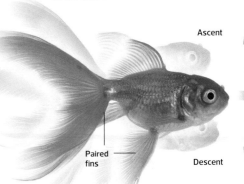

Ascent

Paired fins

Descent

❷ Forceful Stroke

Muscles on both sides of the spinal column, especially the tail muscles, contract in an alternating pattern. These contractions power the wavelike movement that propels the fish forward. The crest of the wave reaches the pelvic and dorsal fins.

The crest of the wave passes to the first dorsal fins.

When the crest reaches the area between the two dorsal fins, the tail fin begins its push to the right.

❸ Complete Cycle

When the tail moves back toward the other side and reaches the far right, the head will once again turn to the right to begin a new cycle.

1 second

The amount of time it takes for this shark to complete one swimming cycle

CAT SHARK
Scyliorhinus sp.

The resulting impulse moves the fish forward.

Swimming in Groups

Only bony fish can swim in highly coordinated groups. Schools of fish include thousands of individuals that move harmoniously as if they were a single fish. To coordinate their motion they use their sight, hearing, and lateral line senses. Swimming in groups has its advantages: it is harder to be caught by a predator, and it is easier to find companions or food.

School

A group of fish, usually of the same species, that swim together in a coordinated manner and with specific individual roles

1 cubic mile
(4 cu km)
The area that can be taken up by a school of herring

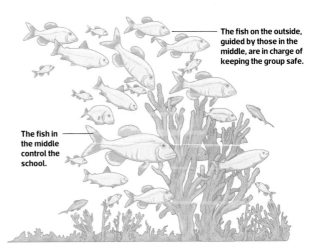

The fish on the outside, guided by those in the middle, are in charge of keeping the group safe.

The fish in the middle control the school.

Wonders of Color

Fish use color to communicate with others of their species. They also use color in mating rituals and even to hide from their prey. A young emperor angelfish has blue and white spirals, but it develops its own appearance when it reaches maturity. This helps it to find a mate and define its territory. Today science is discovering how fish perceive differences of color and what sort of messages the colors convey. ●

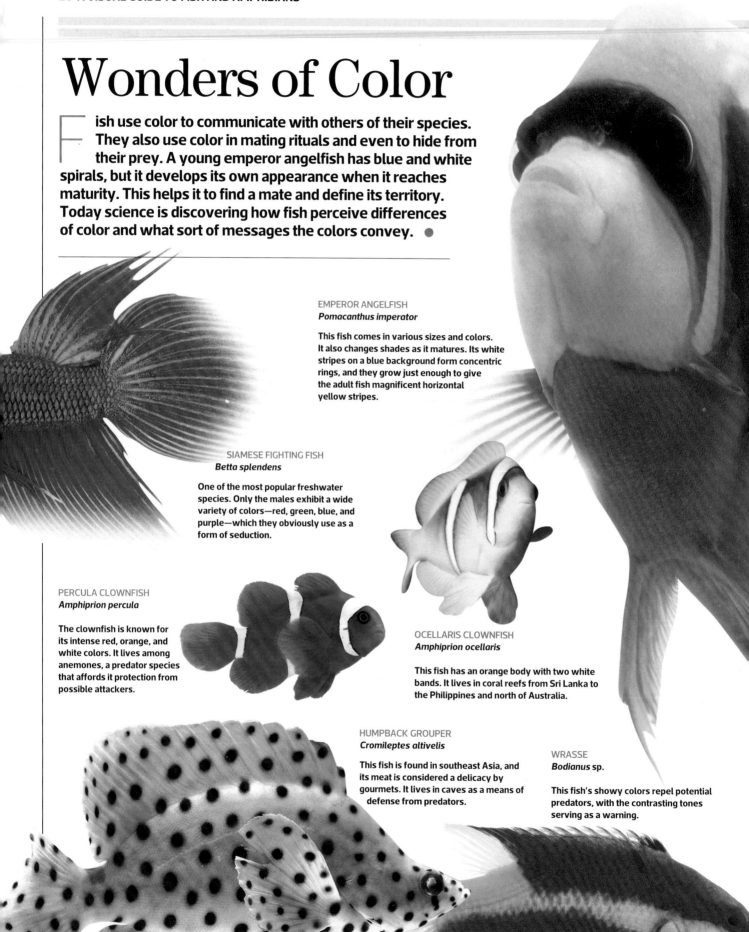

EMPEROR ANGELFISH
Pomacanthus imperator

This fish comes in various sizes and colors. It also changes shades as it matures. Its white stripes on a blue background form concentric rings, and they grow just enough to give the adult fish magnificent horizontal yellow stripes.

SIAMESE FIGHTING FISH
Betta splendens

One of the most popular freshwater species. Only the males exhibit a wide variety of colors—red, green, blue, and purple—which they obviously use as a form of seduction.

PERCULA CLOWNFISH
Amphiprion percula

The clownfish is known for its intense red, orange, and white colors. It lives among anemones, a predator species that affords it protection from possible attackers.

OCELLARIS CLOWNFISH
Amphiprion ocellaris

This fish has an orange body with two white bands. It lives in coral reefs from Sri Lanka to the Philippines and north of Australia.

HUMPBACK GROUPER
Cromileptes altivelis

This fish is found in southeast Asia, and its meat is considered a delicacy by gourmets. It lives in caves as a means of defense from predators.

WRASSE
***Bodianus* sp.**

This fish's showy colors repel potential predators, with the contrasting tones serving as a warning.

CLOWN TRIGGERFISH
Balistoides conspicillum

Half of its body is black with large white spots, and the other half is nearly all black, with a group of strange black shapes with a yellow border. Its bright orange lips look like those of a clown.

GOLDFISH
Carassius auratus

This adaptable fish is the most popular for aquariums. Its highly developed sense of smell is important in its search for mates and food.

WHITETAIL DAMSELFISH
Dascyllus aruanus

With its white body and three thick black stripes, this fish swims among rocks and coral, blending in with its environment.

HARLEQUIN TUSKFISH
Choerodon fasciatus

One of the most brightly colored species of fish in the tropical seas, this fish is endangered by its popularity with aquarium aficionados.

THREADFIN BUTTERFLY FISH
Chaetodon auriga

A dark band covers each eye, and a black eye-shaped spot on its tail fools predators by making them believe the fish is bigger than it really is.

MANDARIN DRAGONET
Synchiropus splendidus

Covered with psychedelic swirls in green, blue, and yellow, this is one of the most beautiful fish on the planet. This small species lives hidden among the rocks of coral reefs.

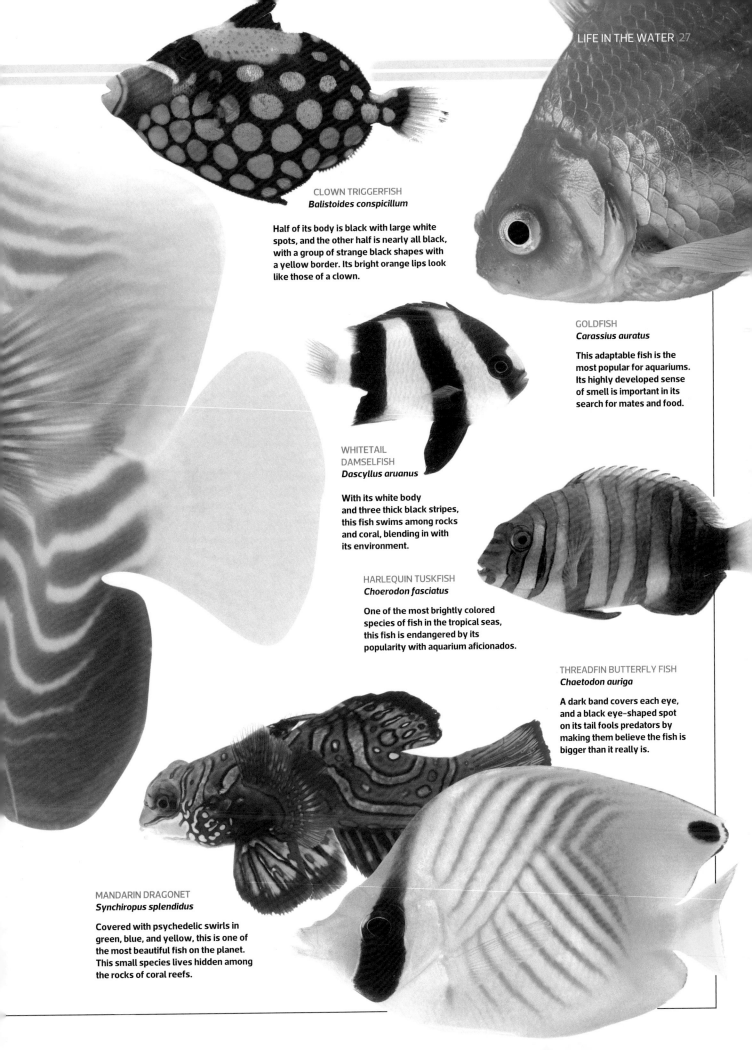

Assortment of Shapes

Most fish have a typical streamlined shape, as exemplified by salmon or trout. Other species have developed widely varying characteristics as adaptations to their environment or diet. The longnose hawkfish has a pronounced proboscis for eating invertebrates on the seabed. The stiff, slender body of the longhorn cowfish causes it to swim slowly and clumsily. And the clown knifefish has a flattened, knifelike body that enables it to move more easily through the water.●

FIRE GOBY
Nemateleotris magnifica

In the Indian and Pacific oceans this fish swims among coral reefs in search of food. Its other name, fire dartfish, comes from its pronounced upright dorsal fin. This small fish is barely the size of a finger.

PRICKLY LEATHERJACKET
Chaetodermis penicilligerus

Inhabiting coral reefs in the tropical waters of the Indian and Pacific oceans, Australia, and northern Japan, this fish can be up to 12 inches (30 cm) long.

SEAWEED PIPEFISH
Syngnathus schlegeli

LONGHORN COWFISH
Lactoria cornuta

inhabits the Pacific Ocean and the Red Sea. Its rigid skeleton makes it a clumsy swimmer in spite of its beautiful silhouette. It has two horns on the upper part of its head.

RED HANDFISH
Brachionichthys politus

Limited to coastal habitats of Australia, this inoffensive fish has an average size of 6 inches (15 cm).

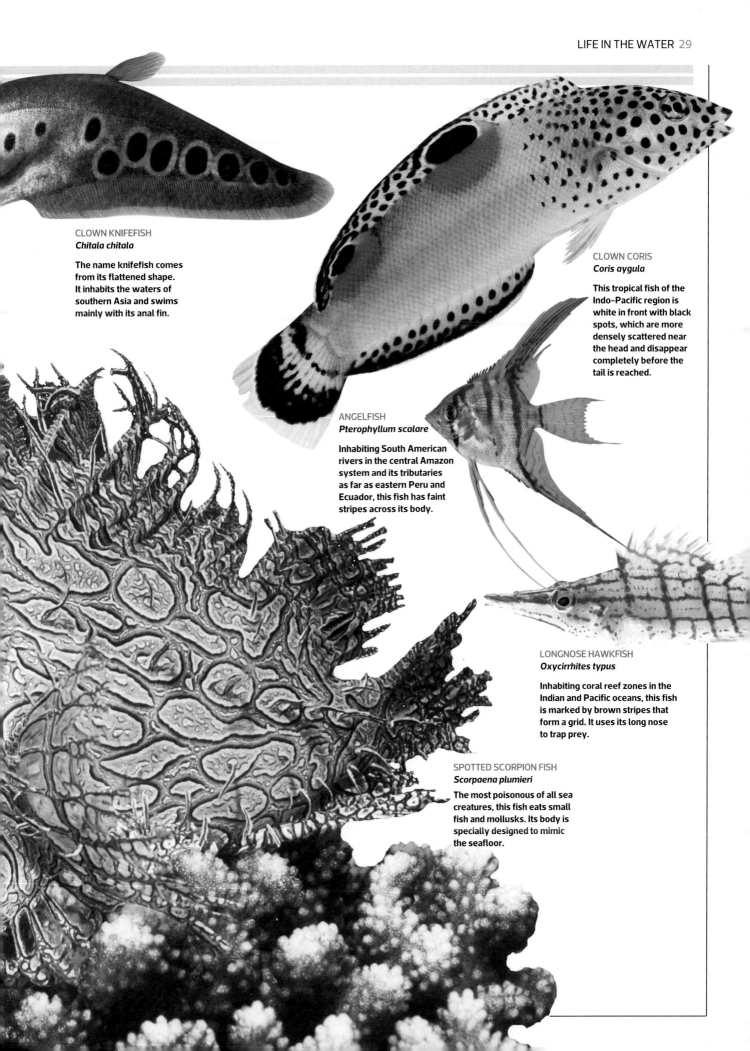

CLOWN KNIFEFISH
Chitala chitala

The name knifefish comes from its flattened shape. It inhabits the waters of southern Asia and swims mainly with its anal fin.

CLOWN CORIS
Coris aygula

This tropical fish of the Indo-Pacific region is white in front with black spots, which are more densely scattered near the head and disappear completely before the tail is reached.

ANGELFISH
Pterophyllum scalare

Inhabiting South American rivers in the central Amazon system and its tributaries as far as eastern Peru and Ecuador, this fish has faint stripes across its body.

LONGNOSE HAWKFISH
Oxycirrhites typus

Inhabiting coral reef zones in the Indian and Pacific oceans, this fish is marked by brown stripes that form a grid. It uses its long nose to trap prey.

SPOTTED SCORPION FISH
Scorpaena plumieri

The most poisonous of all sea creatures, this fish eats small fish and mollusks. Its body is specially designed to mimic the seafloor.

You Are What You Eat

Most fish feed in their natural environment, the larger fish eating the smaller ones, and the smallest sea creatures feeding on marine plants. A fish's mouth gives many clues about its feeding habits. Large, strong teeth indicate a diet of shellfish or coral; pointed teeth belong to a hunting fish; and a large mouth that is open while the fish swims is that of a filterer. Some species can also trap food that lives outside the water: trout, for example, hunt flies. ●

CORAL
Parrotfish feed on corals.

Predators

These are fish that feed on other species. They have teeth or fangs that help them to wound and kill their prey or to hold it fast after the attack. Predators use their sight to hunt, although some nocturnal species such as moray eels use their senses of smell and touch and those of their lateral line. All predators have highly evolved stomachs that secrete acid to digest meat, bones, and scales. Such fish have a shorter intestinal tract than herbivorous species, so digestion takes less time.

MOUTH
acts as a filter. As it swims along with its mouth open, zooplankton and small fish are trapped.

WHALE SHARK
Rhincodon typus

PIRANHA
Pygocentrus sp.

RAZOR-SHARP TEETH
Large, sharp teeth go along with a predator's diet.

Filterers

Some species have evolved to the point of being able to take from the water only those nutrients they need for feeding. They filter the nutrients out using their mouths and gills. These species include whale sharks (*Rhincodon typus*), herring (*Clupea* sp.), and Atlantic menhaden (*Brevoortia tyrannus*).

Symbiosis

is the interaction between two organisms that live in close cooperation. One type of symbiosis is parasitism, in which one organism benefits and the other is harmed. An example of a parasite is the sea lamprey (*Petromyzon marinus*), which sticks to other fish and sucks their body fluids to feed itself. Another type of symbiosis is commensalism, in which one organism benefits and the other is not harmed. An example is the remora (*Remora remora*), or suckerfish, which sticks to other fish using suction disks on the end of its head.

Plants

Life in the water is based on phytoplankton, which is eaten by zooplankton. These are in turn eaten by fish, all the way up to the large marine species.

SUCKERS
They close their eyes, turn them, and push them downward to increase the pressure of the mouth.

REMORA
Remora remora

Grazers

This group of fish eats vegetation or coral in small bites. Parrotfish (Scaridae) have a horny beak made of fused teeth. They scrape the fine layer of algae and coral that covers rocks and then crush it into powder using strong plates in the back of the throat.

FUSED TEETH

Parrotfish have a strong beak that enables them to bite the bony skeleton of corals and eat the algae that grows on them. The beak is actually made of individual teeth, arranged in a beaklike structure.

PHARYNGEAL PLATES

After biting a clump of coral covered with algae, the pharyngeal plates, strong grinding structures in the throat, crush the hard, stony pieces.

DIFFERENCES

Carnivorous fish eat all sorts of species, even though their basic diet consists of meat. They have terminal-type mouths, muscular stomachs, and short intestinal tracts. Herbivores feed on aquatic vegetation. They have a long intestinal tract compared with other fish.

PARROTFISH
Scarus sp.

Types of Mouths

Terminal

Superior

Inferior

Protusible

Suckers

Species that live in the depths, such as sturgeons (Acipenseridae) and suckerfish (Catostomidae), spend their days sucking the mud on the seafloor. When they are cut open, large amounts of mud or sand are found in the stomach and intestines. Digestive mechanisms process all this material and absorb only what is needed.

THE VACUUM

Sucking fish use their mouths like a large vacuum cleaner to hunt their prey.

BARBELS

The sturgeon has a prominent snout. In its mouth it has four sensitive barbels.

STURGEON
Acipenser sp.

Life Cycle

n an underwater environment, animals can simply secrete their sex cells into the water. But for fertilization to be effective, the male and the female must synchronize their activities. Many species, such as the salmon, travel great distances to meet with potential mates. Upon meeting a mate they release their sex cells. The time and place are important because the survival of the eggs depends on the water temperature. Parent–child relations are extremely varied, from complete neglect of the eggs once laid to constant watchfulness and protection of the young. ●

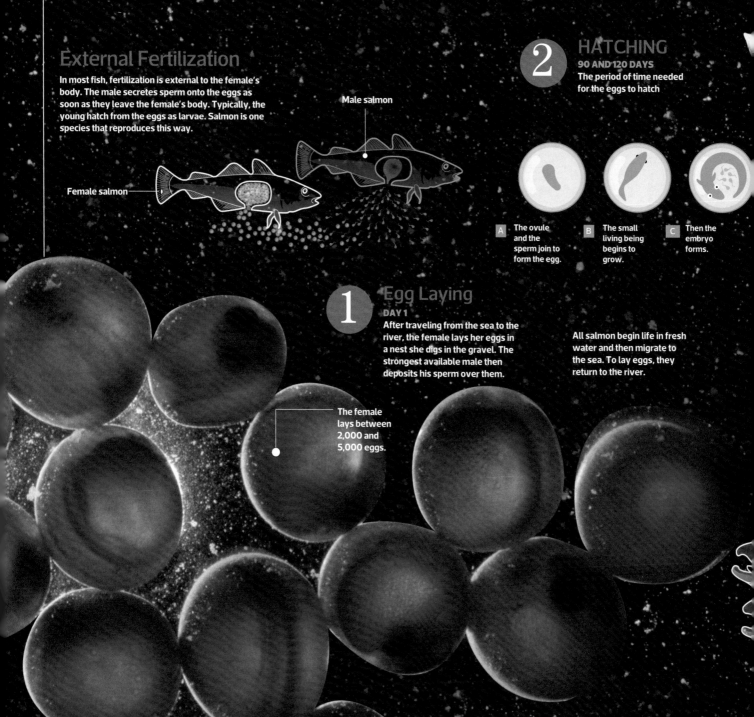

External Fertilization

In most fish, fertilization is external to the female's body. The male secretes sperm onto the eggs as soon as they leave the female's body. Typically, the young hatch from the eggs as larvae. Salmon is one species that reproduces this way.

Male salmon

Female salmon

2 HATCHING

90 AND 120 DAYS
The period of time needed for the eggs to hatch

A The ovule and the sperm join to form the egg.

B The small living being begins to grow.

C Then the embryo forms.

1 Egg Laying

DAY 1
After traveling from the sea to the river, the female lays her eggs in a nest she digs in the gravel. The strongest available male then deposits his sperm over them.

All salmon begin life in fresh water and then migrate to the sea. To lay eggs, they return to the river.

The female lays between 2,000 and 5,000 eggs.

BODY OF THE FRY

3 YOUNG FISH (FRY)

121 DAYS
The small fry feed from the yolk sac.

BODY OF THE FRY

FRY'S YOLK SAC

6 Year Cycle

This is the life span of a salmon.

Parents

The yellow-headed jawfish, *Opisthognathus aurifrons*, incubates its eggs inside its mouth.

Mouth Incubation

The gestation of some fish species takes place inside the parents' mouths. They incubate the eggs inside their mouths and then spit them out into the burrow. Once the eggs hatch, the parents protect their young by sheltering them again inside their mouths.

Internal Fertilization

Viviparous fish give birth to their young in the form of developed juveniles. Fertilization is internal, carried out by a male organ called the gonopod, which is a modified fin.

Ovary

Paraplacental uterine space

Umbilical cord

Placenta

4 Juveniles

2 years
Salmon fry grow until they become small juvenile salmon. They migrate to the sea, where they live for four years.

Young male

5 Adults

6 years
The adult salmon have fully mature reproductive organs, and they return to the river where they were born to lay their eggs.

Young female

Ovary

Urogenital opening

Matters of Life and Death

To survive, most fish need adaptations to enable them to flee from their predators or to find food. The European plaice can lie on the ocean floor with its flat body. Its ivory color makes it almost invisible. The flying fish, on the other hand, developed pectoral fins to lift itself up over the surface of the water and flee its enemies. ●

European Plaice

The European plaice (*Pleuronectes platessa*) is a flat fish with a shape especially designed to allow it to remain motionless on the seafloor. It also provides an example of mimesis. Its two sides are very different. The top side is pigmented with small red spots that camouflage the fish on the seafloor, where it uses its fins to cover itself with sand to hide from predators.

MOUTH

The European plaice's entire body undergoes metamorphosis from its larval state to adulthood. The mouth, however, remains the same.

EUROPEAN
PLAICE
Pleuronectes platessa

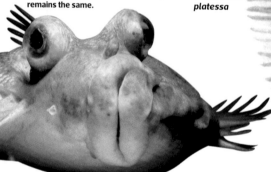

VENTRAL SIDE remains an ivory color, devoid of pigmentation. This side rests on the ocean floor.

SPOTS are useful for camouflage in the sand and for hiding from its predators.

CAUDAL FIN Thin, barely used for swimming.

FIN The dorsal, anal, and caudal fins form a continuous line around the body.

Transformation

At birth, the European plaice does not have a flat form but looks like a normal fish. It eats near the surface and swims using its swim bladder. As time goes by, its body becomes flat. The swim bladder dries up, and the fish sinks to the bottom of the sea.

1 5 days
0.14 inch (3.5 mm)

The vertebrae begin to form.

One eye on each side

45 days
is the amount of time the European plaice takes to become a flat fish from a typical streamlined larva.

2 10 days
0.15 inch (4 mm)

The fold of the fin is forming, and the mouth is already open.

3 22 days
0.31 inch (8 mm)

The left eye moves to the top of the head.

The cleft of the tail develops.

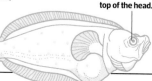

Flying Fish

Exocoetidae, or flying fish, are a family of ocean fish that includes 52 species grouped in eight genera. They are found in all the oceans, especially in warm tropical and subtropical waters. Their most surprising characteristic is their unusually large pectoral fins, which give them the ability to fly and glide for short distances.

1 ESCAPE
When a predator appears, the flying fish propels itself out of the water.

2 TAKEOFF
The fish comes to the surface and elevates itself as high as it can, skipping over the water.

They reach heights of up to **19 feet (6 m)**.

3 GLIDING
The average gliding distance is 160 feet (50 m), but they can glide as far as 660 feet (200 m).

These fish cover distances of up to **160 feet (50 m)** in the air.

Flying fish measure from **7 to 18 inches (18 to 45 cm)** long.

ANATOMY
This fish slides over the water with its hardened fins, and it can reach speeds up to 40 miles per hour (65 km/h) for as long as 30 seconds.

This fish has highly developed pectoral and pelvic fins.

FLYING FISH
Exocoetus volitans

EYES
Both are located on the right side.

Scorpion Fish

Found in the reefs of the Gulf of Mexico, *Scorpaena plumieri*, known commonly as the scorpion fish, has a brown, spotted body with many appendages that look like moss between its mouth and its eyes. This fish is hard to see because its texture and color help it blend easily into the seafloor. Its dorsal fins have a powerful venom, which causes intense pain.

GILLS
The European plaice breathes through its gills.

OPERCULUM
is the bone that supports the gill structure.

SCORPION FISH
Scorpaena plumieri

4 45 days
0.43 inch (11 mm)

The pigment cells join to form dark spots.

It no longer looks to the right, but upward.

The Best Disguise

To face their enemies, fish have developed a number of strategies to enable them to survive. Some of these are escaping, hiding in the ocean bed, or stirring up sand to avoid being seen. Other species have poison, and some can inflate and raise barbs or spines to discourage predators. In the oceans' depths are fish that have luminous organs that blind the enemy. ●

Spot-Fin Porcupine Fish

Like its relative the globefish, this fish swallows water when it feels threatened, swelling up to three times its normal size. This makes it very difficult to fit inside the mouth of a predator. This fish has another defense mechanism: its modified scales act as barbs. When the fish's size increases, the scales extend perpendicularly from the skin.

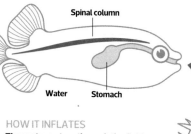

Spinal column

Water   Stomach

HOW IT INFLATES
The water enters through the fish's mouth. The stomach stores water and begins to increase in size. The spinal column and the skeleton are flexible and adapt. If the fish is taken out of the water, it can inflate in a similar way by swallowing air.

The spine curves.

The stomach fills with water.

At Rest
The scales of the porcupine fish lie flat against its body, and its appearance is no different from that of any other bony fish. When it deflates after an attack, it returns to its original state.

Self-Defense
Inflated porcupine fish can reach a diameter of up to 35 inches (90 cm). This makes swallowing them impossible for medium-size predators, which are frightened simply by the porcupine fish's appearance.

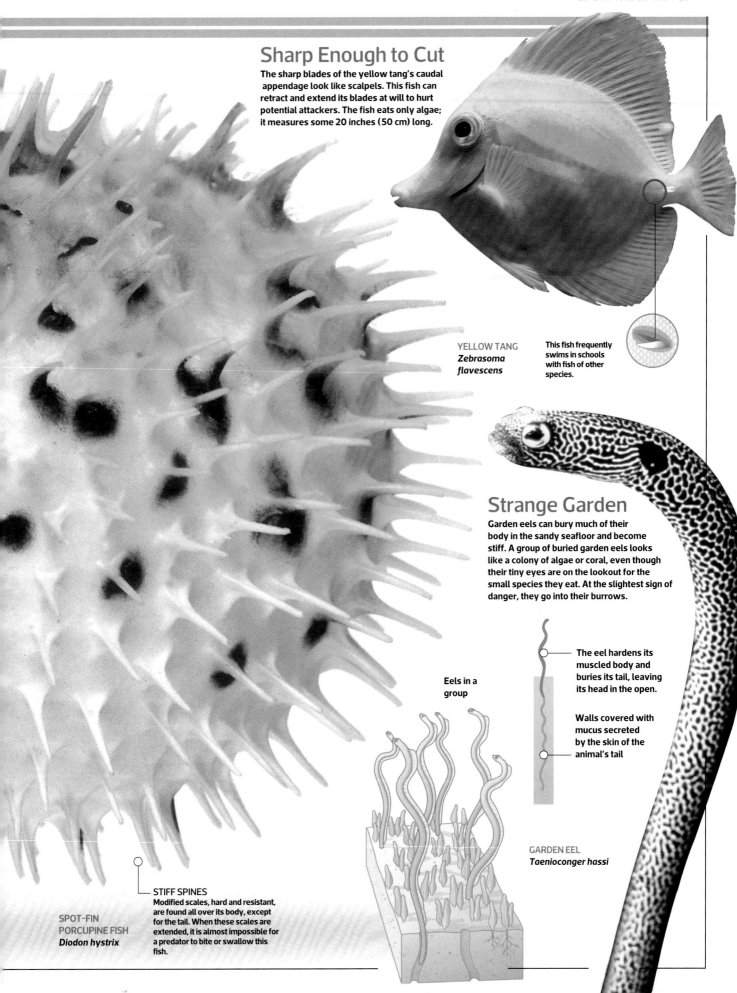

Sharp Enough to Cut

The sharp blades of the yellow tang's caudal appendage look like scalpels. This fish can retract and extend its blades at will to hurt potential attackers. The fish eats only algae; it measures some 20 inches (50 cm) long.

YELLOW TANG
Zebrasoma flavescens

This fish frequently swims in schools with fish of other species.

Strange Garden

Garden eels can bury much of their body in the sandy seafloor and become stiff. A group of buried garden eels looks like a colony of algae or coral, even though their tiny eyes are on the lookout for the small species they eat. At the slightest sign of danger, they go into their burrows.

Eels in a group

The eel hardens its muscled body and buries its tail, leaving its head in the open.

Walls covered with mucus secreted by the skin of the animal's tail

GARDEN EEL
Taenioconger hassi

SPOT-FIN PORCUPINE FISH
Diodon hystrix

STIFF SPINES
Modified scales, hard and resistant, are found all over its body, except for the tail. When these scales are extended, it is almost impossible for a predator to bite or swallow this fish.

Diversity

The ocean depths are inhabited by many types of fish. Some are harmless, but others, such as the scorpion fish, are among the most poisonous creatures in the world. The most feared fish is the great white shark, a true underwater predatory machine—though it seldom attacks humans. In this chapter we will also tell you about the odyssey of

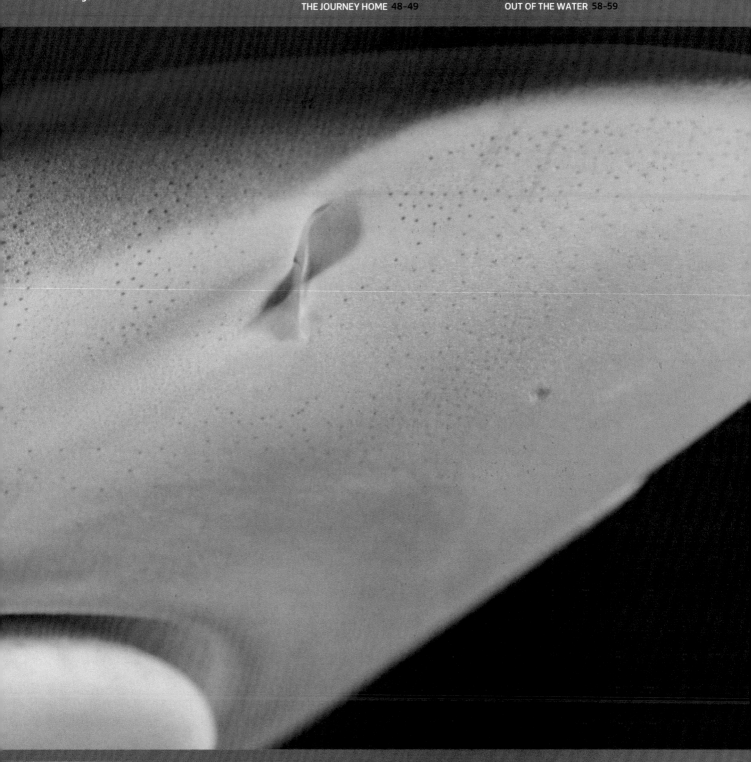

SHARK

To locate its prey, the shark uses several of its senses—smell and hearing over long distances and sight at short range.

many salmon and trout species, which can travel thousands of miles from their ocean home to lay their eggs in the rivers or lakes where they were hatched. The journey lasts from two to three months, and it involves many dangers. It requires so much energy that, after laying their eggs, many females die. ●

Long and Flexible

The seahorse is a small ocean fish that belongs to the same family as pipefish and sea dragons (Syngnathidae). Its name comes from its horselike head. In fact, no other fish genus has its head at a right angle to the rest of its body. Because it cannot use speed to escape from its predators, the seahorse has the ability to change color to blend in with its environment. The reproduction process of these fish is also very unique. The male has an incubating pouch in which the female deposits the fertilized eggs.●

EYES
Large, for acute vision

BLACK-STRIPED PIPEFISH
Syngnathus abaster

One of the slowest fish in the sea, the black-striped pipefish moves by means of slight undulations of its pectoral fins, which can vibrate up to 35 times per second.

Movement

The body of a seahorse is crammed into an armor of large, rectangular bony plates. They swim very differently than other fish. Adopting an upright position, they use their dorsal fin for propulsion. They do not have an anal fin, but rather a long tail that rolls into a spiral. They use it to hold onto underwater plants.

NOSE
Pipe-shaped, giving the head a horselike shape

Classification

Thirty-two species of seahorse have been identified worldwide. Classifying them is at times complicated because individuals of the same species can change color and develop long filaments of skin. The size of adult seahorses varies enormously, from the tiny *Hippocampus minotaur*—a species discovered in Australia that never grows beyond 0.7 inch (1.8 cm) long—to the enormous *Hippocampus ingens*, a species in the Pacific that reaches over 12 inches (30 cm) long. It has no pelvic or caudal fins, but it does have a tiny anal fin.

HEAD

TRUNK
The body is supported by the spinal column.

WEEDY SEA DRAGON
Phyllopteryx taeniolatus

Its shape is typical of this family, although its tail is not suitable for grasping, like those of seahorses are, and it has a more elongated profile. Its body is covered with seaweed.

ROLLED UP
The tail rolls up into a curl.

GRASPING TAIL
With their long tails, seahorses can cling to plants on the seafloor.

UNROLLED
The tail straightens out by unrolling.

TAIL
Can be extended to a fully vertical position

SEAWEED
The fish lets it stick to its body so that it can escape detection.

Camouflage

Since they cannot use speed to escape from predators, seahorses and dragon fish use camouflage as a defense strategy. They change color to blend in with their environment, grow skin filaments shaped like seaweed, and use their heads to climb along the seaweed in which they live, swinging from one plant to another.

LINED SEAHORSE
Hippocampus erectus

Habitat	Caribbean, Indo-Pacific Ocean
Number of species	35
Size	7-12 inches (18-30 cm)

GILLS
Seahorses
breathe through
gills.

35 species

of seahorses live in the
Caribbean, the Pacific Ocean,
and the Indian Ocean.

PECTORAL FIN
One on each
side, for lateral
movement

0.4 inch
(1 cm)

The size of a
seahorse at birth

BONY PLATES
Its body is covered
with concentric
rings of bone.

DORSAL FIN
Seahorses swim
upright, propelled by
their dorsal fin.

Reproduction

The male has an incubating pouch in which the
female deposits her eggs. The sac closes, and
the embryos develop, nourished by the male.
He later expels the young, now mature and
independent, through a series of contractions.

1 During the mating season the female lays
some 200 eggs in the male's pouch using
her egg-depositing organ. There the eggs
are fertilized. When the time for birth arrives,
the male clings to seaweed with his tail.

2 The male bends his body backward and
forward, as if having contractions. The sac's
opening widens, and the birthing process
begins. Soon the young begin to appear.

3 As the male's belly contracts, the young
seahorses are gradually born. Each one
is 0.4 inch (1 cm) long. They begin to
feed on phytoplankton right away. The
birthing process can last two days, after
which the male is exhausted.

Elegant Contours

The Rajiformes are an order of cartilaginous fish related to sharks; they have the same skeletal structure, the same number and type of fins, and similarly shaped gill slits. Rajiformes are distinct in that their gill slits are on the underside of the body, which is flat with pectoral fins joined to the trunk in the shape of a disk. The body is usually covered with denticles, and many have a row of dorsal spikes. They have a variety of colors, with spots and blotches. They often burrow into the mud of warm seas. ●

Tail   Pectoral fin

RAYS
Raja sp.

Head

Flying Through the Water

▶ Unlike most fish, rays have weak, slender tails that do little to power their swimming. They move with their enormous pectoral fins, which are joined to the head and have a characteristic rhomboid shape. Their movement rises and falls in an S curve, as if they were flying underwater.

POISONOUS TAIL
has a dangerous stinger.

BLUE LINES
run along the whole length of the tail.

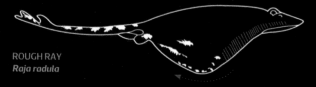

ROUGH RAY
Raja radula

PECTORAL FINS
are joined to the body just behind the head near the gills.

TAIL
is slender and lacks the strength for swimming.

12.4 miles per hour
(20 km/h)

Blue-spotted Ribbontail Ray

Its body is covered with blue spots. It inhabits reefs, caves, and crevices. Its tail has a powerful stinger that injects venom into predators when it feels threatened.

Smiling Face

▶ The ray's face is unique. It is protected by a flap on the underside of its body. Its hornlike mouth is adapted for grasping crustaceans, and the five gill slits on each side are for breathing underwater.

LITTLE SKATE
Raja erinacea

Nasal orifices

Hornlike mouth

Gill arch

FINS
move up and down during swimming.

HEAD
remains upright, looking forward.

THERE ARE
ABOUT

300

SPECIES OF RAJIFORMES

BLUE-SPOTTED
RIBBONTAIL RAY
Taeniura lymma

Habitat	Indian and Pacific oceans
Diet	Crustaceans
Length	Up to 6.6 feet (2 m)
Poisonous	Yes

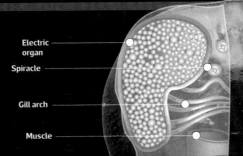

Electric organ
Spiracle
Gill arch
Muscle

Electric Ray

Electric rays (*Torpedo* sp.) are highly active fish with electric organs on each side of the head. Each electric organ is made of numerous disk-shaped cells, connected in parallel. When all the cells fire at once, an electric current is discharged into the water at 220 volts, enough to stun the prey.

TAIL WITH ELECTRIC CHARGE

PELVIC FINS
Small in size

EYES
Turned outward

PECTORAL FINS
Joined to the head

COMPARED FOR SIZE
The manta ray is the largest in the world. In spite of its large size, it is harmless, feeding only on sea plankton.

23 feet (7 m)

MANTA
RAY

Weight 3,300
pounds (1,500 kg)

8.2 feet (2.5 m)

BUTTERFLY
RAY

3.3 feet (1 m)

THORNBACK
RAY

Row of teeth

Nasal orifices

Mouth

Sawfish

Fish of the order Pristiformes have long bodies with an unmistakable face, adorned with 32 pairs of denticles on each side. The females give birth to 15 to 20 young, which are born with a protective membrane over their teeth to keep from hurting the mother.

Deadly Weapon

O ne of the greatest predators in the ocean is the great white shark, easily identified by its distinctive white coloring, black eyes, and fierce teeth and jaws. Many biologists believe that attacks on humans result from the shark's exploratory behavior, because these fish often lift their heads above the water and explore things by biting them. This activity is often dangerous because of the sharpness of the sharks' teeth and the strength of their jaws. Great white sharks are implicated in most fatal shark attacks on humans, especially on surfers and divers.

Senses

Sharks have senses that most animals lack. The ampullae of Lorenzini are small clefts in the shark's head that detect electricity. This sense helps them find prey hidden in the sand. The lateral line is used to detect movement or sound underwater. Smell is their most advanced sense, and it occupies two thirds of their brain. They also have a highly developed sense of hearing, which allows them to detect very low-frequency sounds.

SHARK ATTACKS 1876-2004

- 23 MEDITERRANEAN
- 84 WEST COAST OF U.S.
- 8 EAST COAST OF U.S.
- 2 JAPAN
- 1 SOUTH KOREA
- 1 MEXICO
- 3 SOUTH AMERICA
- 47 SOUTH AFRICA
- 41 AUSTRALIA
- 10 NEW ZEALAND

220 ATTACKS IN 128 YEARS

Hearing
Detects sounds of very low frequency

Ampulla of Lorenzini
Detects nerve impulses

Nose
The most highly developed sense is smell; it takes up two thirds of the brain.

Lateral line detects movements or sounds underwater.

Electric radar

DORSAL FIN

ANAL FIN

CAUDAL FIN
The great white shark has a large heterocercal caudal fin.

PELVIC FIN

PECTORAL FIN
Highly developed and very important for swimming

GREAT WHITE SHARK
Carcharodon carcharias

Habitat	Oceans
Weight	4,400 pounds (2,000 kg)
Length	23 feet (7 m)
Life span	30–40 years

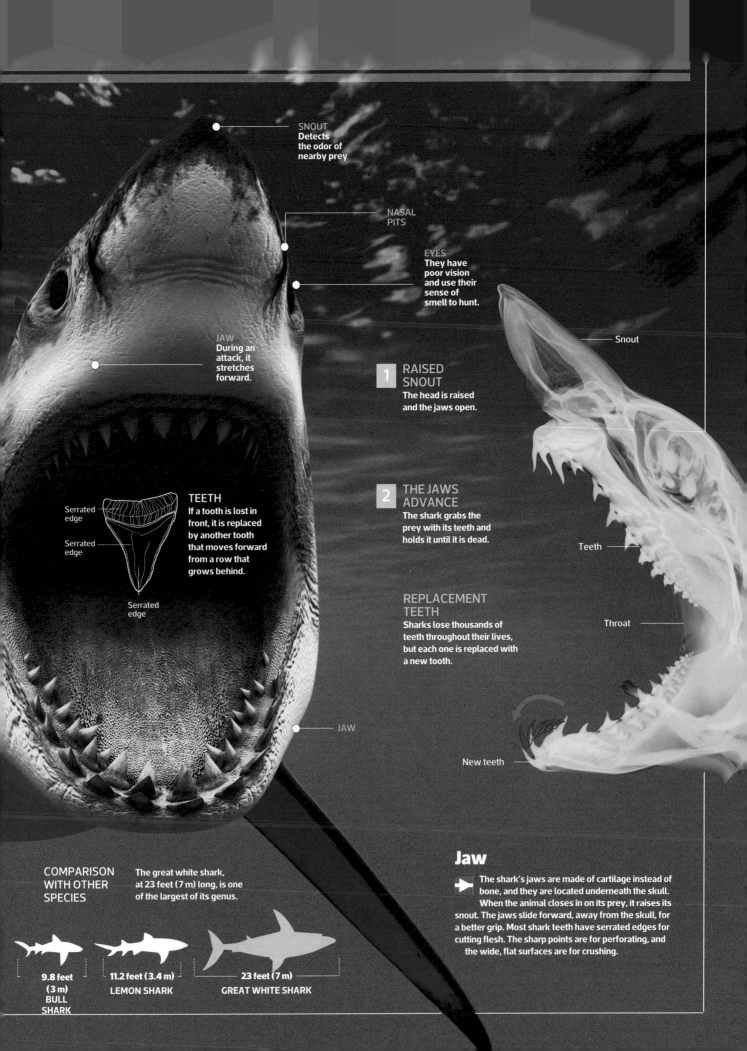

SNOUT
Detects the odor of nearby prey

NASAL PITS

EYES
They have poor vision and use their sense of smell to hunt.

JAW
During an attack, it stretches forward.

TEETH
If a tooth is lost in front, it is replaced by another tooth that moves forward from a row that grows behind.

Serrated edge

Serrated edge

Serrated edge

1 RAISED SNOUT
The head is raised and the jaws open.

2 THE JAWS ADVANCE
The shark grabs the prey with its teeth and holds it until it is dead.

REPLACEMENT TEETH
Sharks lose thousands of teeth throughout their lives, but each one is replaced with a new tooth.

JAW

Snout

Teeth

Throat

New teeth

COMPARISON WITH OTHER SPECIES

The great white shark, at 23 feet (7 m) long, is one of the largest of its genus.

9.8 feet (3 m) BULL SHARK

11.2 feet (3.4 m) LEMON SHARK

23 feet (7 m) GREAT WHITE SHARK

Jaw

The shark's jaws are made of cartilage instead of bone, and they are located underneath the skull. When the animal closes in on its prey, it raises its snout. The jaws slide forward, away from the skull, for a better grip. Most shark teeth have serrated edges for cutting flesh. The sharp points are for perforating, and the wide, flat surfaces are for crushing.

Time to Eat

Most fish feed within their aquatic environment. Some species, however, seek their food outside the water. The best-known example is the archerfish, which shoots streams of water from its mouth to knock spiders and flies off nearby plants and into the water. The African butterfly fish eats flying insects, which it traps after a brief flight. The river hatchetfish has a similar strategy: its long pectoral fins and flattened body enable it to make great leaps. ●

Archerfish

Seven species of archerfish live in the tropical waters of India and southeast Asia. They hunt using an unusual technique of spitting streams of water.

9.4 inches (24 cm)

3.1 inches (8 cm)

Technique

The tongue presses upward against a groove in the roof of the mouth, forming a tube for emitting the stream of water.

Groove in roof of mouth

Movement of tongue

The tongue acts as a valve to keep the water under pressure.

Angle of vision

Archerfish have large eyes and excellent vision for hunting.

90°

EXACT ANGLE OF VISION

At an angle close to 90° to the surface of the water, it focuses on the prey.

In a vertical position, it sees the prey well enough to attack it.

5 feet (1.5 m)

Range of the water stream for an adult fish

4 inches (10 cm)

Range of the water stream for a young fish

Strategy

The carnivorous archerfish has developed a special strategy for hunting live insects, which is highly effective for hunting prey outside the water at distances of up to 5 feet (1.5 m).

It looks at the prey and shoots a stream of water.

When the insect falls into the water, the fish devours it.

A SEARCH
The archerfish looks upward in search of its prey.

B SHOT
When it finds its prey, the archerfish positions its body upright and shoots a stream of water at the target.

C AIM
If the first stream misses, the fish tries again and again.

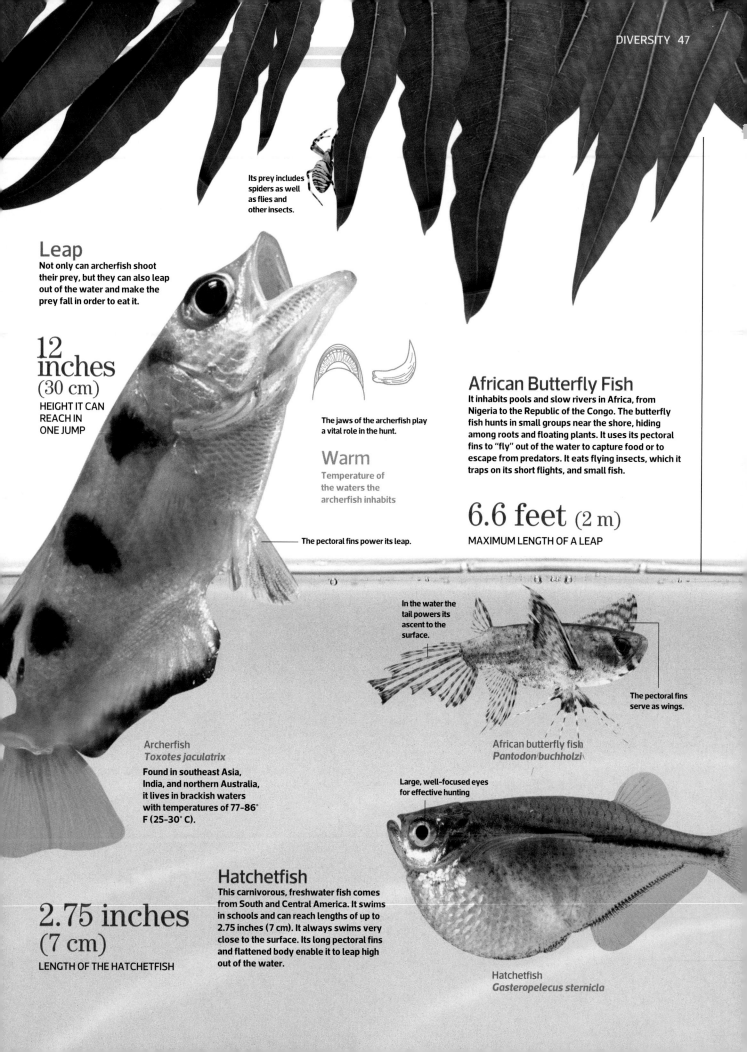

Its prey includes spiders as well as flies and other insects.

Leap

Not only can archerfish shoot their prey, but they can also leap out of the water and make the prey fall in order to eat it.

12 inches (30 cm)
HEIGHT IT CAN REACH IN ONE JUMP

The jaws of the archerfish play a vital role in the hunt.

Warm
Temperature of the waters the archerfish inhabits

The pectoral fins power its leap.

African Butterfly Fish

It inhabits pools and slow rivers in Africa, from Nigeria to the Republic of the Congo. The butterfly fish hunts in small groups near the shore, hiding among roots and floating plants. It uses its pectoral fins to "fly" out of the water to capture food or to escape from predators. It eats flying insects, which it traps on its short flights, and small fish.

6.6 feet (2 m)
MAXIMUM LENGTH OF A LEAP

In the water the tail powers its ascent to the surface.

The pectoral fins serve as wings.

Archerfish
Toxotes jaculatrix

Found in southeast Asia, India, and northern Australia, it lives in brackish waters with temperatures of 77–86° F (25–30° C).

African butterfly fish
Pantodon/buchholzi

Large, well-focused eyes for effective hunting

Hatchetfish

This carnivorous, freshwater fish comes from South and Central America. It swims in schools and can reach lengths of up to 2.75 inches (7 cm). It always swims very close to the surface. Its long pectoral fins and flattened body enable it to leap high out of the water.

2.75 inches (7 cm)
LENGTH OF THE HATCHETFISH

Hatchetfish
Gasteropelecus sternicla

The Journey Home

After living in the ocean for five or six years, the Pacific red salmon (*Oncorhynchus nerka*) returns to the river where it was born to reproduce. The journey lasts from two to three months, and it demands a great deal of energy. The salmon must swim against the current, climb waterfalls, and evade predators, including bears and eagles. Once the salmon reach the river, the female lays her eggs, and the male fertilizes them. Typically, the same locations in specific rivers are sought year after year. This species of salmon dies after completing the reproductive cycle, unlike the Atlantic salmon, which repeats the cycle three or four times. Once the eggs hatch, the cycle begins anew. ●

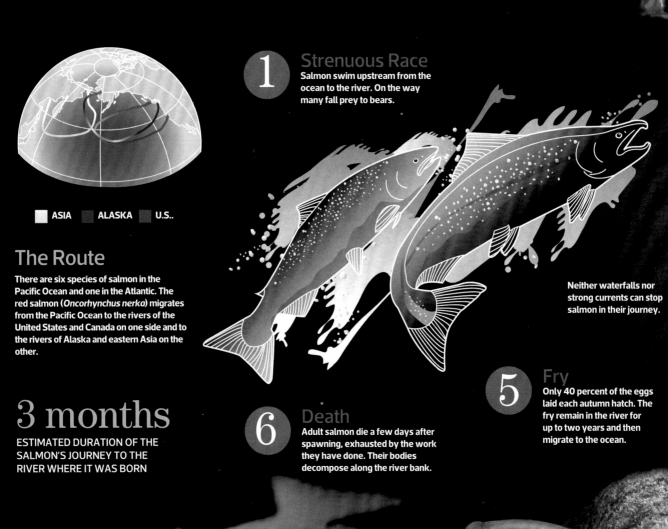

ASIA   ALASKA   U.S..

The Route

There are six species of salmon in the Pacific Ocean and one in the Atlantic. The red salmon (*Oncorhynchus nerka*) migrates from the Pacific Ocean to the rivers of the United States and Canada on one side and to the rivers of Alaska and eastern Asia on the other.

3 months

ESTIMATED DURATION OF THE SALMON'S JOURNEY TO THE RIVER WHERE IT WAS BORN

1 Strenuous Race
Salmon swim upstream from the ocean to the river. On the way many fall prey to bears.

Neither waterfalls nor strong currents can stop salmon in their journey.

5 Fry
Only 40 percent of the eggs laid each autumn hatch. The fry remain in the river for up to two years and then migrate to the ocean.

6 Death
Adult salmon die a few days after spawning, exhausted by the work they have done. Their bodies decompose along the river bank.

Survival

Of the more than 7,500 eggs that two females can lay, only two hatched fish will remain at the end of the life cycle of two years. Many eggs die before hatching, and after hatching, salmon fry are easy prey for other fish.

Eggs		7,500
Fry		4,500
Fry		650
Fry		200
Salmon		50
Adult Salmon		4
Egg Spawning		2

2 Red River

The salmon returns to its birthplace to spawn. Males have intense coloration with a green head.

3 The Couple

While females are busy preparing nests in the sand to deposit their eggs, males compete for mates.

5,000
QUANTITY OF EGGS A FEMALE CAN LAY

Seen from above, salmon appear as a large red spot.

MOUTH
During mating season, the lower jaw of the male curves upward.

BACK
A hump develops in the dorsal section of the body.

6-Year Cycle
LENGTH OF TIME FROM SPAWNING TO ADULTHOOD

COLOR
The blue-backed salmon turns a fiery red.

4 Spawning

The female deposits between 2,500 and 5,000 eggs in a series of nests. The male fertilizes them as they fall between the rocks.

Habitat, Tastes, and Preferences

The oceans cover 70 percent of the Earth's surface. That is where life began on this planet and where the most primitive species live side by side with the most highly evolved ones. This abundance of species is due in part to the wide variety of environments found in the ocean. As one descends in depth, the water's temperature decreases, as does the amount of light. These factors determine different ecosystems, feeding regimes, and adaptation strategies among a wide variety of fish species. ●

Reserve of Life

Corals need warm water and lots of light. They are colonies of polyps that secrete a calcareous substance that form great reefs over the years. The resulting microhabitat harbors a great variety of species.

REEFS form only in very shallow tropical waters.

0–650 feet (0–200 m)

Epipelagic Zone
Algae and the animals that eat them inhabit this zone, where photosynthesis is possible because of the presence of sunlight.

490 feet (150 m)

At this depth there is no plankton. Many species that live below this depth swim above it at night to feed.

30 feet (9 m)
Divers without special equipment

50 feet (15 m)
Pearl divers

160 feet (50 m)
Scuba divers

PLANKTON
Herbivorous fish can be found only in shallow waters because of the presence of plankton there.

Swordfish

Hammerhead Shark

Manta Ray

Snapper

Cod

Flying Fish

Trumpet Fish

Clownfish

Sergeant Fish

Blue Angelfish

Barracuda

Striped Perch

Pacific Sardines

Moray Eel

Ocean Sunfish

Tiger Shark

Puffer Fish

1,150 feet (350 m)
S.P. 350 saucer of Cousteau

1,300 feet (400 m)
JIM diving suit (1970)

3,000 feet (915 m)
Barton bathosphere (1960)

5,000 feet (1,525 m)
Submarine rescue vehicle

12,500 feet (3,810 m)
Deep submergence vehicle Alvin

19,800 feet (6,000 m)
MIR (Russia)

21,500 feet (6,500 m)
Shinkay (Japan)

36,000 FEET
(10,911 M)

FATAL LIGHT
Predators of the deep use their bioluminescence to attract their prey.

TO SEE WITHOUT LIGHT
As a form of adaptation, the retinas of these carnivores are sensitive only to the color blue, which is the color that propagates best in water.

The Greatest Depth

The bathyscape *Trieste* holds the record for the maximum depth achieved by any submarine vehicle. In 1960 it descended into the Mariana Trench to 36,000 feet (10,911 m) below sea level and withstood the tremendous pressure at that depth.

Spotted Eagle Fish

Eel

Red Starry Ray

Giant Grouper

Dragonfish

Football Fish

Bonefish

Pineapple Fish

Sixgill Shark

Marine Serpent

California Slickhead

Gulper Eel

Toadfish

Angel Shark

Butterfly Fish

Queenfish

Fangtooth (Ogrefish)

Tripod Fish

650–3,300 feet
(200–1,000 m)

Mesopelagic Zone
Not enough light is found at this depth to allow algae to live.

2,000 feet
(600 m)

No light whatsoever reaches this depth.

BOTTOM FEEDERS
At any given depth of the ocean floor, bottom feeders can be found wallowing in the mud searching for food.

3,300–13,000 feet
(1,000–4,000 m)

Bathypelagic Zone
Species that inhabit this zone do so in complete darkness, except for those creatures that are bioluminescent, generating their own light. Temperature varies between 35° and 40° F (2° and 4° C).

Below
13,000 feet
(4,000 m)

Abyssopelagic Zone
Scarcely explored. There are some large fish with strong teeth and other species, such as sea sponges and starfish.

HEAT FOR LIFE
Volcanic vents are the only source of heat. They make it possible for the forms of life found near them to exist.

Volcanoes

In some abyssal plains volcanic phenomena take place that constitute a catalyst for life. Lava from the volcanoes cools quickly, solidifies, and forms chimneys around which an explosion of microscopic (bacterial) and macroscopic (infaunal worms) life occurs that can serve as food for various species of fish.

Minerals

Solidified Lava

Magma Chamber

Danger in the Water

There are poisonous fish in all the seas in the world. The toxic substances they produce are usually not meant for threatening humans but for defending themselves from larger aquatic predators. Although some species of puffer fish have poisonous flesh, in Japan they are considered a delicacy when properly prepared. ●

A Swimming Fortress

Red lionfish, also called scorpion fish, are fascinating sea creatures found in aquariums all over the world. They belong to the family Scorpaenidae, which includes fish that have spines and venom, such as the spotted scorpion fish. The dorsal fin of the red lionfish has spines containing small sacs of potent venom, which it uses in self-defense. It has a long body with high, wide fins. The potency of the venom depends on the species.

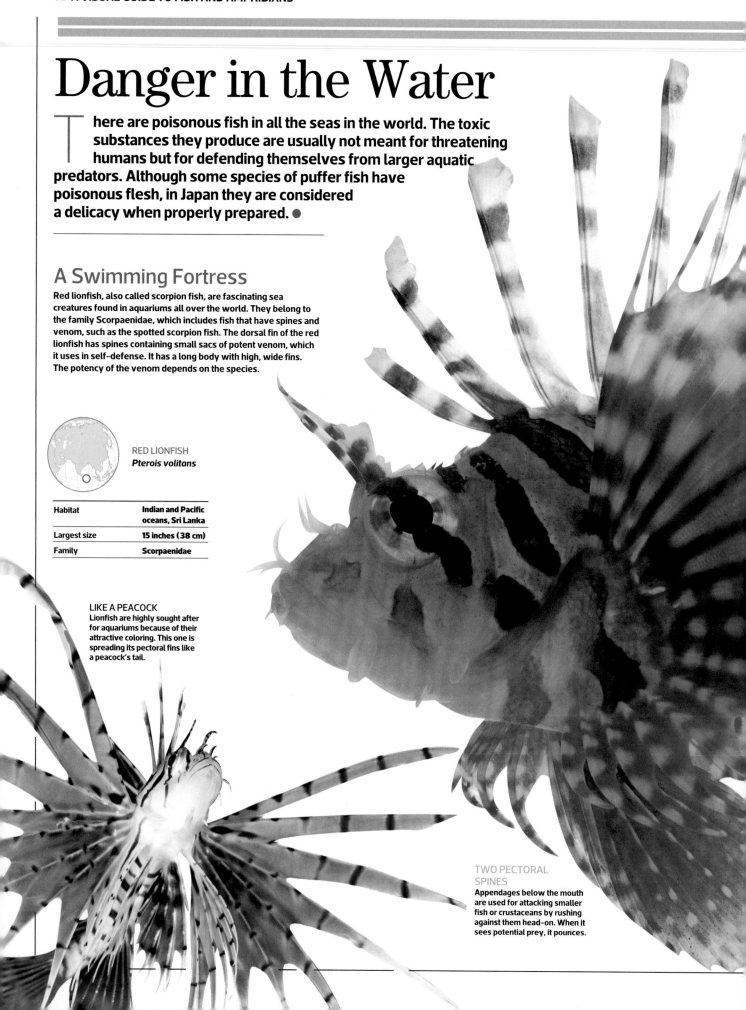

RED LIONFISH
Pterois volitans

Habitat	Indian and Pacific oceans, Sri Lanka
Largest size	15 inches (38 cm)
Family	Scorpaenidae

LIKE A PEACOCK
Lionfish are highly sought after for aquariums because of their attractive coloring. This one is spreading its pectoral fins like a peacock's tail.

TWO PECTORAL SPINES
Appendages below the mouth are used for attacking smaller fish or crustaceans by rushing against them head-on. When it sees potential prey, it pounces.

Deadly Weapons

Each spine is covered from base to tip with a sheath. When the spine pierces, the pressure causes the poison gland within to release its contents.

THIRTEEN DORSAL SPINES

The fiercer the attack, the more damaging are the wounds they inflict. They can do worse damage if the spine breaks and sticks in the victim's body.

Covering

Poison gland

Spine of fin

Base of spine

The poison gland lies along the inside of a long central groove and is covered with glandular tissue that secretes the venom.

Deadly Delicacy

In Japan the fugu, or puffer fish, is a succulent but lethal delicacy. It contains tetratoxin, a deadly poison. Nonetheless, its flesh is so delicious that Japanese gourmets, even at the risk of their lives, consider fugu the king of fish. To prepare this high-risk dish, chefs must have a certificate from a special school that teaches the preparation of fugu.

INTESTINE
The puffer fish's intestinal wall is also poisonous.

OVARY
The most toxic of the internal organs

STOMACH
When the fish takes in water, the stomach swells and causes the fish to expand.

LIVER
Highly poisonous; compressed when the stomach expands

CAUDAL FIN
Its showy colors frighten predator species with the coded message: "I'm poisonous!"

Living Rock

Spotted scorpion fish belong to another group of the Scorpaenidae family. Buried in the sand along ocean beaches, their strong, thick spines can pierce footwear when stepped on. They can live up to four months eating only the fish that swim near their mouths.

Pressure on the spines opens the sacs of poison. Through channels in the middle of the spines, the poison is injected into deliberate or accidental aggressors.

Poisonous spines

SPOTTED SCORPION FISH
Scorpaena plumieri

THREE ANAL SPINES

The first three spines of the anal fin point downward.

1,200 times

The relative potency of the venom of a puffer fish compared with cyanide. This gives an idea of its killing potential.

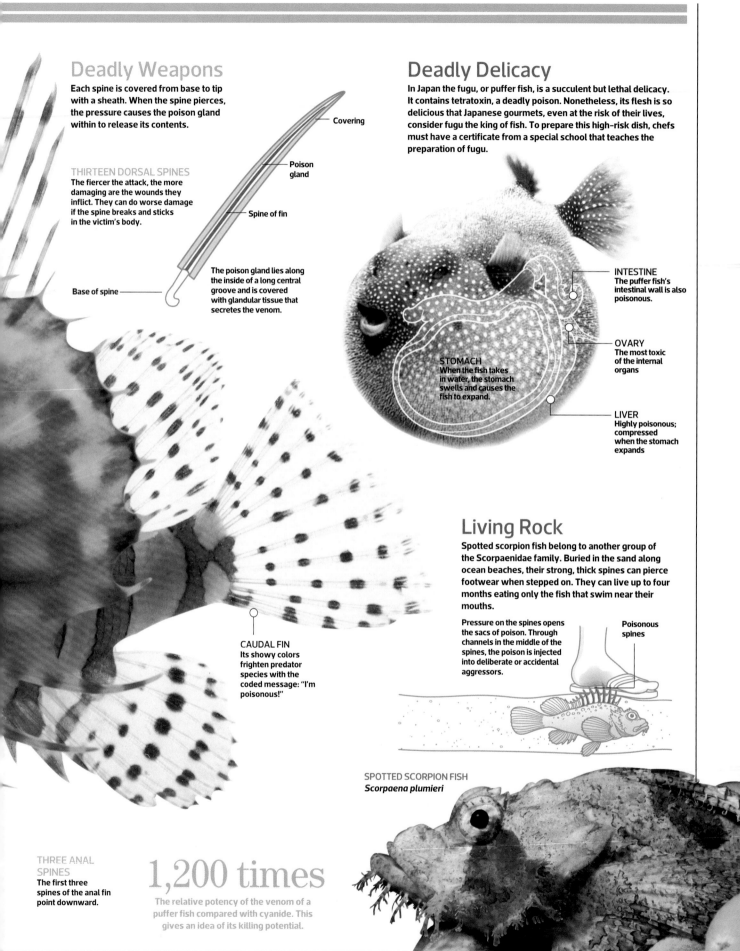

Kings of Darkness

n depths below 8,200 feet (2,500 m), where barely any light penetrates, live rare species known as abyssal fish. In this environment, life is possible near hydrothermal vents in the seafloor that warm the nearby waters. In spite of this natural warmth, in many areas the temperature never rises above 36° F (2° C). At this depth fish have peculiar shapes, with large heads and strong teeth for eating other fish, since no vegetation can grow there. To attract their prey, many have "lure" organs made of photophores that shine in the darkness. They also are usually black or dark brown for purposes of camouflage.

SHARP, POINTED TEETH
It gulps down its prey after grabbing them with its enormous teeth and its strong suction force.

SLOANE'S VIPERFISH
Chauliodus sloani
Between 12 and 20 inches (30 and 50 cm) in stature, it is dark blue or silvery in color and lives in warm tropical waters.

LANTERN
Like most abyssal fish, it has a lure organ.

EYES FOR SEEING IN DIM LIGHT

TAPETUM
reflects light like a mirror. Each ray hits the retina twice, doubling its sensitivity.

RAY OF LIGHT

RETINA
Blind to red light. It registers only blue light waves, which travel better in the water.

FANGTOOTH
Anoplogaster cornuta
This fearsome hunter kills its prey by seizing it with its jaw and strong teeth.

FANFIN SEADEVIL
Caulophryne jordani
This dark-brown fish uses the photophore organ on its head to penetrate the darkness.

FILAMENTS
cover its entire body for protection.

FUMAROLE
Openings in the Earth's surface that discharge geothermal water and minerals. As the water cools, these minerals solidify.

36°F (2°C)
Temperature of water heated by fumaroles

DRAGONFISH
Bathophilus sp.
Found in most tropical regions of the world, it has photophores along both sides of its body.

TUBE WORM TENTACLES
Tube worms have neither mouths nor digestive tracts. They feed on organic molecules formed from elements in the water by chemosynthetic bacteria that live inside the worms.

CHIN APPENDAGE
Shines in the darkness

LANTERN
produces bluish light, which reaches farthest underwater.

1.1 tons (1,000 kg)

1.3 cubic yards (1 cu m) of water

=

GLOWING LURE
Produces light to attract prey

DIMENSIONS

Weight 10.6 ounces (300 g)

4 inches (10 cm)

SKIN
Dark colors are likely to make it invisible to attackers.

HUMPBACK ANGLERFISH
Melanocetus johnsonii
6 inches (15 cm) long. Its small fins are insufficient to enable fast maneuvering.

HYDROSTATIC PRESSURE
The weight of the column of water. The pressure of the water increases with depth. In the Mariana Trench (the deepest undersea trench on the planet), every square centimeter bears the weight of 1.2 tons (7.7 tons per square inch) of water.

8,200 feet (2,500 m)
Depth of water

KILLER JAWS
In the ocean's depths, only the best hunter survives.

BODY
Black, to avoid being seen by predators.

ILLUMINATED NETDEVIL
Linophryne arborifera
has a glowing lure on the end of its nose and a branching beard that also glows to attract prey. The male is smaller than the female and lives off of her like a parasite.

CHIN APPENDAGE
Produces light to attract prey

GLOWING LURE
gives off light to attract prey.

TAILS AND FINS
contain luminous cells.

ATLANTIC FOOTBALL FISH
Himantolophus groenlandicus
The females can reach up to 24 inches (60 cm) long, whereas the males barely reach 1.6 inches (4 cm) long and live as parasites on their mates.

Sea Snakes

Eels (Anguilliformes), an order of ray-finned fish (Actinopterygii), are distinctive for their elongated, snakelike shape. In the past they were an important food source. There are about 600 species of true eels, including morays, congers, and snake eels. Eels come in a wide variety of colors and patterns, ranging from solid gray to mottled yellow. Their bodies lack scales and are covered with a protective mucous membrane. One of the most striking eels is the green moray, which lives in the Caribbean Sea and hides in coral reefs awaiting its prey. Although it is not poisonous, it is feared by divers because its bite can inflict grave wounds. ●

GREEN MORAY
Gymnothorax funebris

Habitat	Caribbean Sea
Depth	25-200 feet (8-60 m)
Weight	64 pounds (29 kg)

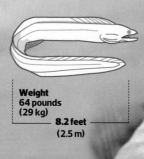

**Weight
64 pounds
(29 kg)**
**8.2 feet
(2.5 m)**

Green Moray

Unlike most fish, the moray has no scales. It excretes a slippery film to cover its thick, muscular body and protect itself from parasites. The moray hunts at night and detects its prey with its excellent sense of smell.

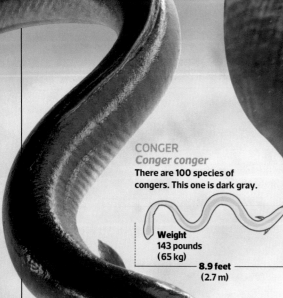

CONGER
Conger conger
There are 100 species of congers. This one is dark gray.

**Weight
143 pounds
(65 kg)**
**8.9 feet
(2.7 m)**

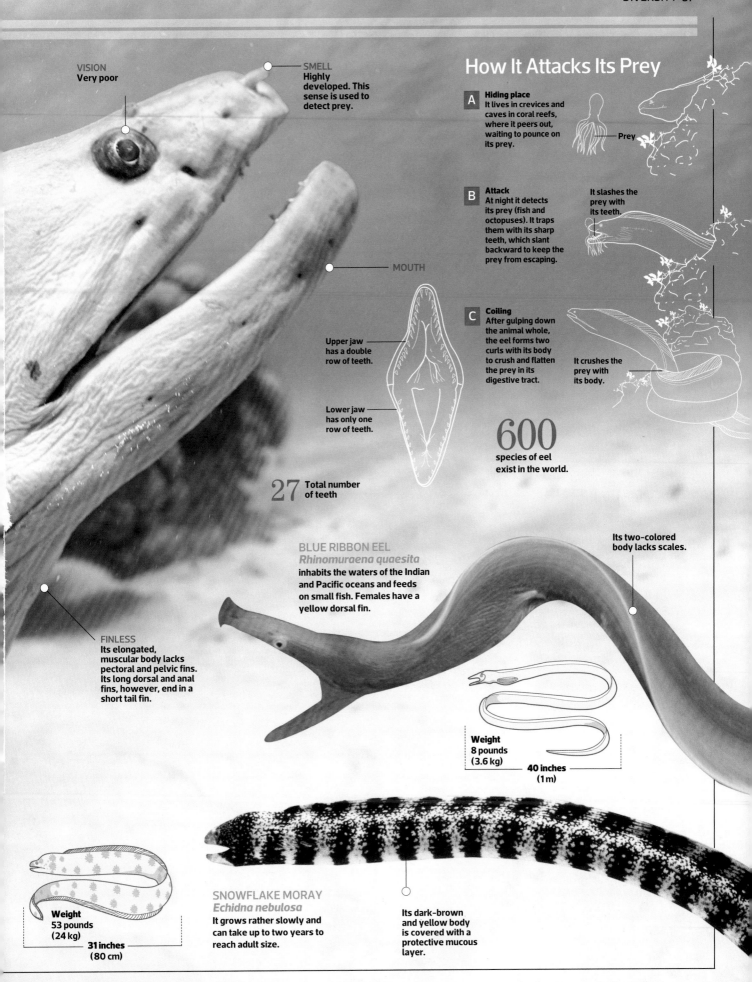

VISION
Very poor

SMELL
Highly developed. This sense is used to detect prey.

How It Attacks Its Prey

A **Hiding place**
It lives in crevices and caves in coral reefs, where it peers out, waiting to pounce on its prey.

Prey

B **Attack**
At night it detects its prey (fish and octopuses). It traps them with its sharp teeth, which slant backward to keep the prey from escaping.

It slashes the prey with its teeth.

C **Coiling**
After gulping down the animal whole, the eel forms two curls with its body to crush and flatten the prey in its digestive tract.

It crushes the prey with its body.

MOUTH

Upper jaw has a double row of teeth.

Lower jaw has only one row of teeth.

600
species of eel exist in the world.

27 Total number of teeth

BLUE RIBBON EEL
Rhinomuraena quaesita
inhabits the waters of the Indian and Pacific oceans and feeds on small fish. Females have a yellow dorsal fin.

Its two-colored body lacks scales.

FINLESS
Its elongated, muscular body lacks pectoral and pelvic fins. Its long dorsal and anal fins, however, end in a short tail fin.

Weight
8 pounds
(3.6 kg)

40 inches
(1 m)

SNOWFLAKE MORAY
Echidna nebulosa
It grows rather slowly and can take up to two years to reach adult size.

Its dark-brown and yellow body is covered with a protective mucous layer.

Weight
53 pounds
(24 kg)

31 inches
(80 cm)

Out of the Water

Some species of fish can breathe and live out of the water. They include the mudskippers in southeast Asia, which can stay on muddy flats and even climb trees. To breathe, they need only their skin to stay moist, thanks to the function of certain cells in their skin. A few other species still have rudimentary lungs like those of the first aquatic animals that colonized dry land.●

Fish with Lungs

Lungfish have rudimentary lungs that originate from a connection between the swim bladder and the esophagus. This allows the swim bladder to function using air when the fish leaves the water. Depending on the species, the fish can breathe air occasionally or even indefinitely. Many varieties of these fish have been found in fossil form all over the world, which indicates that they were very widespread during the Mesozoic Era. They were probably the first vertebrates to develop lungs. However, lungfish species are found in only three areas today, all in freshwater environments.

SOUTH AMERICAN LUNGFISH
Lepidosiren paradoxa

has a small gill apparatus and two lungs with which it breathes during the dry season.

WEST AFRICAN LUNGFISH
Protopterus annectens annectens

has fleshy fins that look like limbs and three external gills. In the dry season it secretes a substance for covering itself. It can remain in this state for up to a year.

9 months
Length of time certain lungfish can live buried in the mud

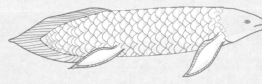

QUEENSLAND LUNGFISH
Neoceratodus forsteri

When forced to breathe air for long periods, this fish will die. It can reach up to 50 inches (1.25 m) long, weigh 22 pounds (10 kg), and live more than 65 years.

1 WATER LEVELS DROP
The fish looks for an area with soft mud under the water, where it can easily dig itself a burrow.

2 HEAD FIRST
On entering the burrow head first, the fish secretes thick mucus, which enables it to slide in easily and also protects it from dehydration.

3 TURNING AROUND
The lungfish curls in on itself with its head up. Before the water level drops, it seals the entry with a plug of clay.

4 HIBERNATION
The fish breathes through two or three small holes in the plug. Its bodily functions are reduced to a minimum.

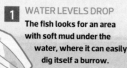

Some water is still left in the pond.

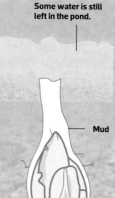

Mud

The water has receded completely.

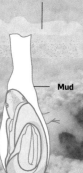

Mud

In the Mud

When the dry season arrives, and rivers and ponds dry up, both the African and South American species of lungfish dig holes in the mud along the shore and bury themselves. They then reduce their metabolic functions to a minimum and burn as little energy as possible until the waters rise again.

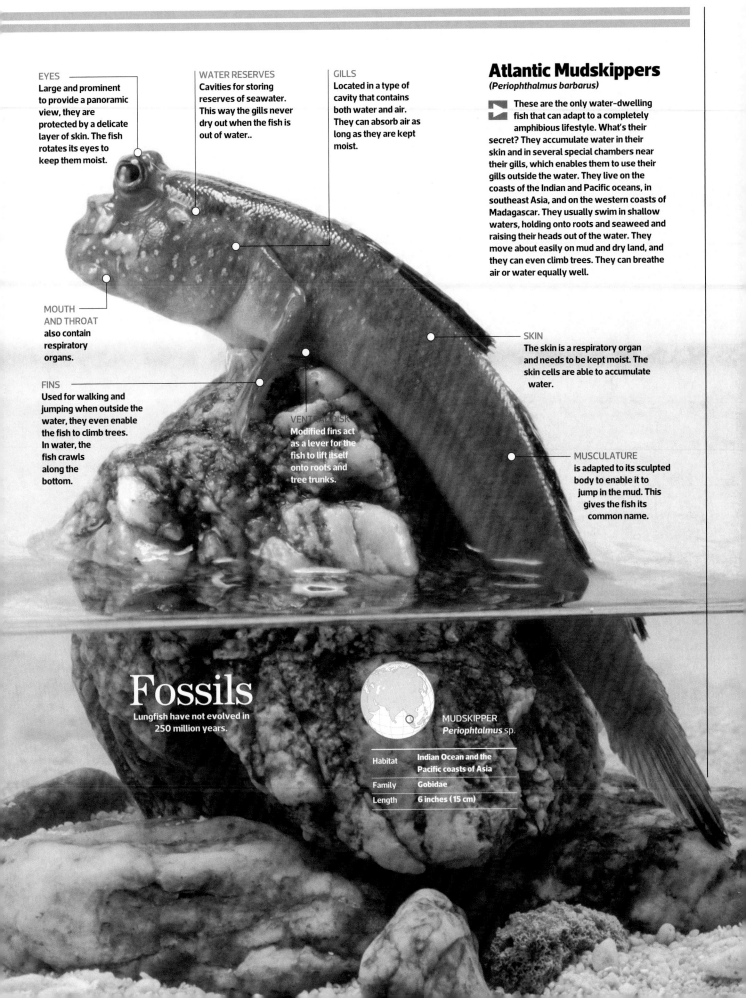

EYES
Large and prominent to provide a panoramic view, they are protected by a delicate layer of skin. The fish rotates its eyes to keep them moist.

WATER RESERVES
Cavities for storing reserves of seawater. This way the gills never dry out when the fish is out of water..

GILLS
Located in a type of cavity that contains both water and air. They can absorb air as long as they are kept moist.

MOUTH AND THROAT
also contain respiratory organs.

FINS
Used for walking and jumping when outside the water, they even enable the fish to climb trees. In water, the fish crawls along the bottom.

VENTRAL DISK
Modified fins act as a lever for the fish to lift itself onto roots and tree trunks.

Atlantic Mudskippers
(Periophthalmus barbarus)

These are the only water–dwelling fish that can adapt to a completely amphibious lifestyle. What's their secret? They accumulate water in their skin and in several special chambers near their gills, which enables them to use their gills outside the water. They live on the coasts of the Indian and Pacific oceans, in southeast Asia, and on the western coasts of Madagascar. They usually swim in shallow waters, holding onto roots and seaweed and raising their heads out of the water. They move about easily on mud and dry land, and they can even climb trees. They can breathe air or water equally well.

SKIN
The skin is a respiratory organ and needs to be kept moist. The skin cells are able to accumulate water.

MUSCULATURE
is adapted to its sculpted body to enable it to jump in the mud. This gives the fish its common name.

Fossils
Lungfish have not evolved in 250 million years.

MUDSKIPPER
Periophtalmus sp.

Habitat	Indian Ocean and the Pacific coasts of Asia
Family	Gobidae
Length	6 inches (15 cm)

Amphibians

Few groups of amphibians have generated as much scientific interest as frogs of the genus Dendrobates, which produce toxic secretions through their skin. All frogs of this genus have spectacular coloring to warn their predators of the danger. One of the most important traits of amphibians (newts, salamanders, frogs, toads, and

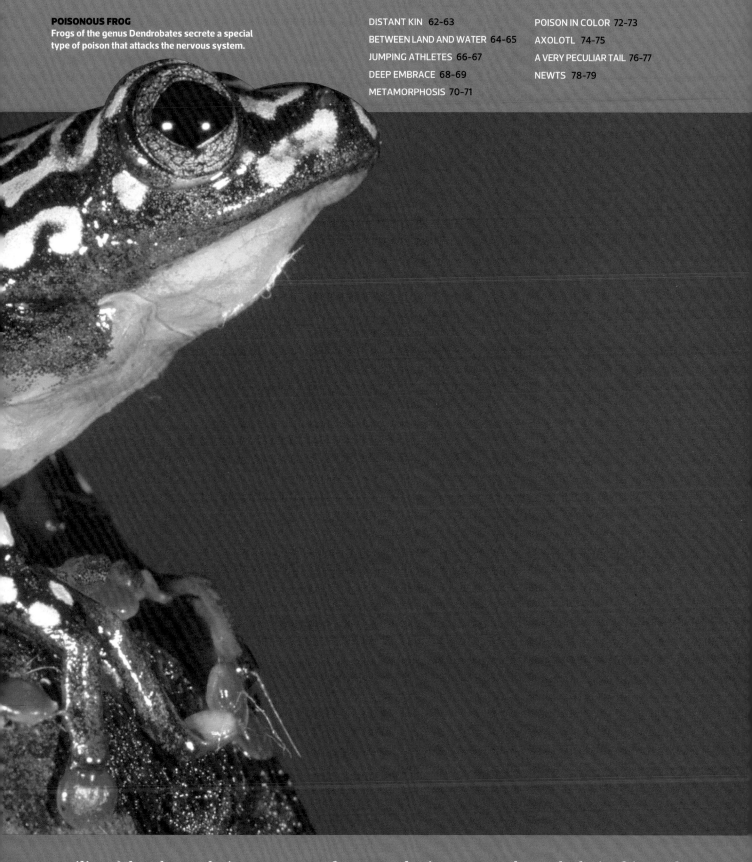

POISONOUS FROG
Frogs of the genus Dendrobates secrete a special
type of poison that attacks the nervous system.

caecilians) has been their conquest of
land. This completely transformed the
extremities of these animals, allowing
them to move on land instead of
swimming. They also had to adapt to
take in oxygen through their skin and
lungs. Here you will also discover how
frogs and toads reproduce and how
newts feed, among other curious facts. ●

Distant Kin

The first amphibians evolved from fish with fleshy, lobed fins that resembled legs. They may have been attracted to land as a source for food, but the most important reason for their leaving the water was the instability of the Devonian Period, which drastically affected freshwater environments. During long droughts, the fish used their fleshy fins to move from one pond to another. Oxygen availability was also affected, and this led to more organisms being able to breathe oxygen from the air. ●

Legs: Evolution

In 2004, American paleontologist Neil Shubin of the University of Chicago offered the scientific community a complete description of a humerus bone that was 365 million years old. The first tetrapods adapted to land exhibited a great variety of leg shapes, sizes, and strengths. After comparing this fossil with that of other tetrapods, scientists concluded that the evolution of the legs and of the muscles necessary for walking began in the water.

Tiktaalik

A lobe-finned fish from the late Devonian Period, with many tetrapod characteristics. It lived 375 million years ago. Some paleontologists suggest that it was another intermediate form between fish and amphibians.

Eusthenopteron

A relatively large fish, about 29 inches (75 cm) long. Many features of its skeleton were similar to those of the first amphibians; it had a cranial pattern similar to *Acanthostega* and *Ichtyostega*. The skeleton of its fins included a humerus, ulna, and radius in the front fin and a femur, tibia, and fibula in the pelvic fin.

GLYPTOTEPIS

LEGS
They were very similar to aquatic vertebrates.

Rays of skin

Ulna
Radius
Humerus
EUSTHENOPTERON

Rays of skin
Ulna
Humerus
PANDERICHTHYS
Radius

Humerus
Ulna
ACANTHOSTEGA
Radius

ICHTHYOSTEGA
Humerus
Ulna
Radius
Seven toes

Three-lobed tail — **Pelvic fin** — **Muscled pectoral fin**

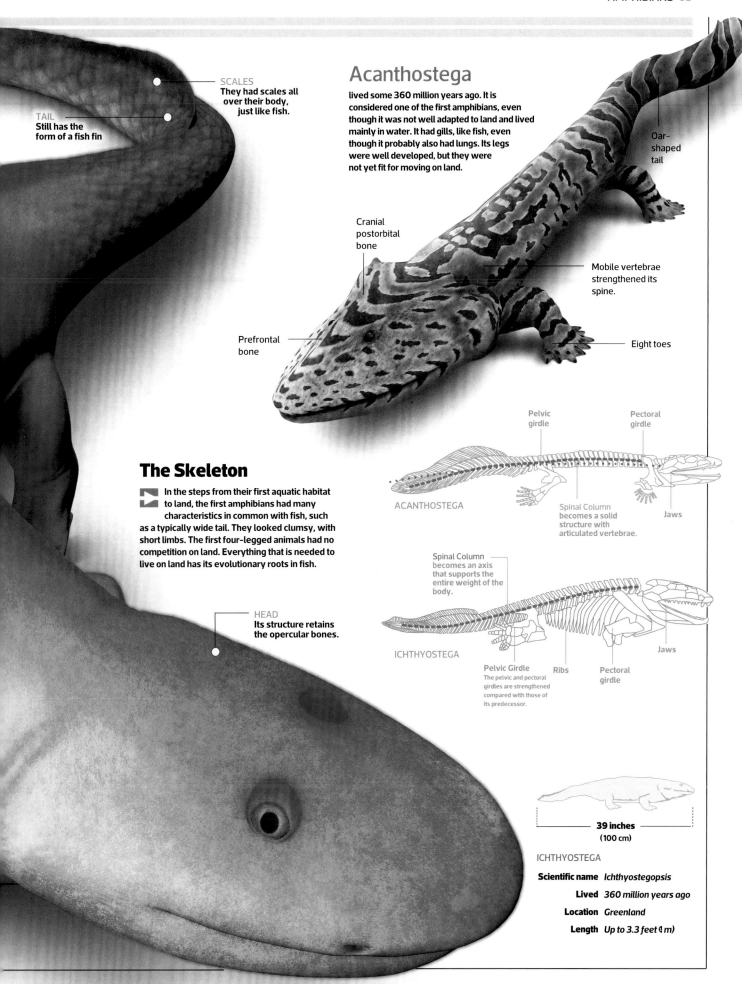

Acanthostega

lived some 360 million years ago. It is considered one of the first amphibians, even though it was not well adapted to land and lived mainly in water. It had gills, like fish, even though it probably also had lungs. Its legs were well developed, but they were not yet fit for moving on land.

SCALES
They had scales all over their body, just like fish.

TAIL
Still has the form of a fish fin

Oar-shaped tail

Cranial postorbital bone

Mobile vertebrae strengthened its spine.

Prefrontal bone

Eight toes

The Skeleton

In the steps from their first aquatic habitat to land, the first amphibians had many characteristics in common with fish, such as a typically wide tail. They looked clumsy, with short limbs. The first four-legged animals had no competition on land. Everything that is needed to live on land has its evolutionary roots in fish.

HEAD
Its structure retains the opercular bones.

Pelvic girdle

Pectoral girdle

ACANTHOSTEGA

Spinal Column becomes a solid structure with articulated vertebrae.

Jaws

Spinal Column becomes an axis that supports the entire weight of the body.

ICHTHYOSTEGA

Pelvic Girdle
The pelvic and pectoral girdles are strengthened compared with those of its predecessor.

Ribs

Pectoral girdle

Jaws

39 inches
(100 cm)

ICHTHYOSTEGA

Scientific name	*Ichthyostegopsis*
Lived	*360 million years ago*
Location	*Greenland*
Length	*Up to 3.3 feet (1 m)*

Between Land and Water

As indicated by their name (*amphi*, "both," and *bios*, "life"), these animals lead a double life. When young, they live in the water, and when they become adults they live outside it. In any case, many must remain near water or in very humid places to keep from drying out. This is because amphibians also breathe through their skin, and only moist skin can absorb oxygen. Some typical characteristics of adult frogs and toads include a tailless body, long hind limbs, and large eyes that often bulge. ●

Amphibian Anatomy

Amphibian anatomy has several peculiarities. Larvae, such as tadpoles, have a respiratory system with gills. Most species develop lungs when they reach adulthood. They also have a trachea, pharynx, and saclike lungs, even though skin breathing is at times more important than lung breathing. The heart has two auricles and one ventricle, and the digestive and excretory systems are similar to those of mammals.

VOCAL SACS

Both toads and frogs sing. Even though the sound is produced by their vocal cords, in males the sound is amplified by means of inflatable sacs on each side of the larynx.

The Skin

Amphibians breathe through their skin, which is clean and smooth, without hair or scales. They must always keep it moist, because it has a strong tendency to dry out. Even though they have mucous glands that help maintain moisture, amphibians must live in damp places. The skin of most amphibians protects them from possible predators and has poisonous glands that secrete unpleasant and even toxic substances.

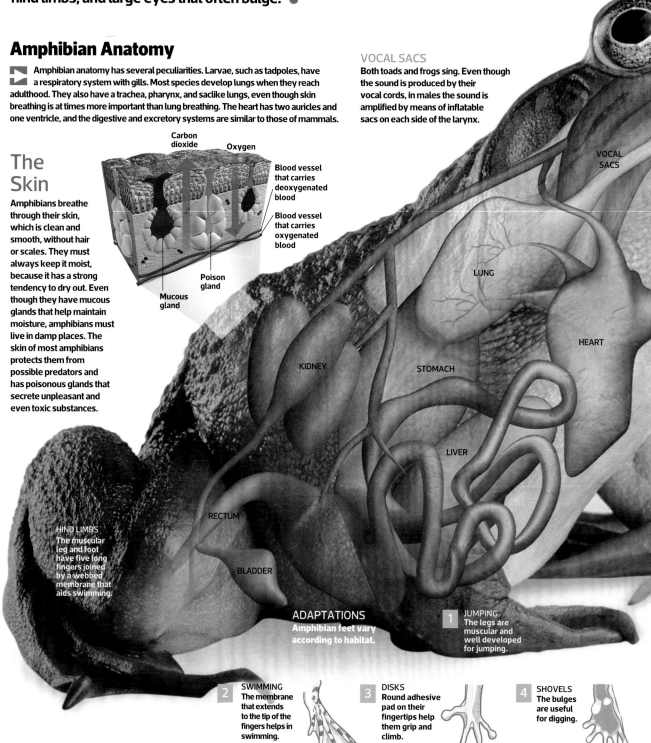

Carbon dioxide

Oxygen

Blood vessel that carries deoxygenated blood

Blood vessel that carries oxygenated blood

Poison gland

Mucous gland

VOCAL SACS

LUNG

HEART

KIDNEY

STOMACH

LIVER

RECTUM

BLADDER

HIND LIMBS
The muscular leg and foot have five long fingers joined by a webbed membrane that aids swimming.

ADAPTATIONS
Amphibian feet vary according to habitat.

1 JUMPING
The legs are muscular and well developed for jumping.

2 SWIMMING
The membrane that extends to the tip of the fingers helps in swimming.

3 DISKS
Round adhesive pad on their fingertips help them grip and climb.

4 SHOVELS
The bulges are useful for digging.

Differences Between Frogs and Toads

It is very common to use "frog" and "toad" as synonyms or to think that the frog is a female toad. However, frogs and toads are quite different. Toads have wrinkled skin and short legs, and they are land animals. Frogs are smaller, have webbed feet, and live in the water and in trees.

SKIN
Soft and smooth, with strong, bright colors

EYES
Frogs have horizontal pupils.

EYES
The pupil is usually horizontal, though some toads have vertical pupils.

SKIN
The skin of a toad is wrinkled, hard, rough, and dry. It is also used as leather.

COMMON TOAD
Bufo bufo

REED FROG
Hyperolius tuberilinguis

POSTURE
Toads are terrestrial species, slow-moving and wider than frogs. Frogs live mainly in water, which is why they have webbed toes adapted for swimming.

LEGS
are long and are adapted for jumping. Frogs have webbed toes to help with swimming.

LEGS
are shorter and wider than those of frogs and are adapted for walking.

CATCHING
Toads gulp down their prey, swallowing it whole.

SWALLOWING
Eye retraction, where the toad closes and turns its eyes inward, increases the pressure in the mouth, pushing food down the esophagus.

Nutrition

is based on plants during the larval stage, whereas in the adult stage the main food sources are arthropods (such as insects of the order Coleoptera and arachnids) and other invertebrates, such as butterfly caterpillars and earthworms.

Types of Amphibians

Amphibians are divided into three groups that are differentiated on the basis of tail and legs. Newts and salamanders have tails. They belong to the order Urodela. Frogs and toads, which have no tail except as tadpoles, belong to the Anura group. Caecilians, which have no tail or legs, are similar to worms and belong to the Apoda group.

ANURA
Tailless

EUROPEAN TREE FROG
is docile and lives near buildings.

APODA
Without legs

RINGED CAECILIAN
looks like a large, thick worm.

Legs

Frogs and toads have four fingers on each front leg and five on each hind leg. Water frogs have webbed feet; tree frogs have adhesive disks on the tips of their fingers to hold on to vertical surfaces; and burrowing frogs have callous protuberances called tubercules on their hind legs, which they use for digging.

TIGER SALAMANDER
One of the most colorful in America

URODELA
With a tail

Jumping Athletes

Amphibians of the order Anura are known for their ability to jump high and far. This group includes frogs and toads, and their anatomy helps them to jump. Frogs use their jumping ability to escape from their many predators; they can jump a distance equivalent to 10 to 44 times their body length. When they feel threatened, they can choose to jump into the nearest body of water, where they hide, or they can jump erratically on land to confuse their attacker. ●

Feeding

2

Amphibians from the order Anura have a varied diet. They feed on insects and small invertebrates such as earthworms, snails, crustaceans, and spiders. Tadpoles are herbivores.

EYES
During the jump the eyes remain shut.

VISIBLE HUMP

The Frog

Its large eyes help it to locate prey easily. The eyes have lids that protect them from particles in the air or help them see underwater. The frog's smooth skin has glands that moisten it or that secrete toxic or irritating substances. The frog breathes through its lungs and skin. It has a large tympanum, or eardrum, visible on each side of the head and a wide mouth that may or may not have teeth.

1

Jumping

Before the jump begins, the frog tenses the muscles of its hind legs and presses its feet against the ground. As the frog jumps, the legs extend to propel the body forward.

STRETCHED-OUT BODY

LEG MUSCLES
tense to carry out the jump.

EDIBLE FROG
Rana esculenta
is found in Europe and also in the United States, Canada, and Asia.

HIND FEET
have five webbed toes.

The Toad

Having characteristics similar to those of frogs, toads can be distinguished by only a few features. Generally, toads are larger, less stylized, and better adapted to living on land. Toads' skin is thicker than that of frogs to prevent drying, and toads are normally covered with warts.

ASIAN TREE FROG
Pedostibes tuberculosus

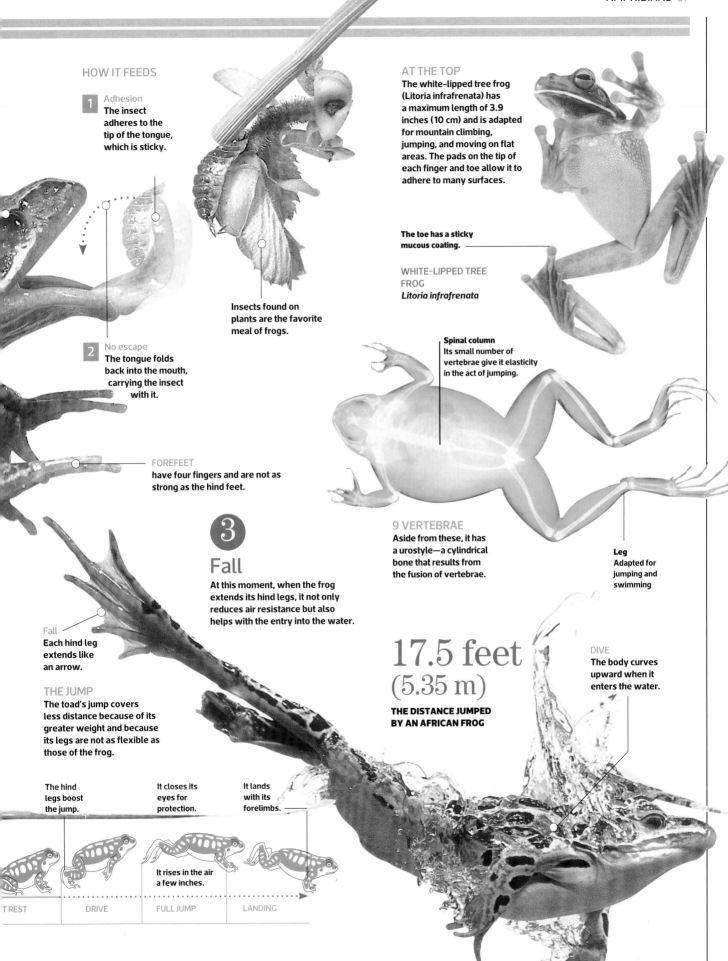

HOW IT FEEDS

1 Adhesion
The insect adheres to the tip of the tongue, which is sticky.

2 No escape
The tongue folds back into the mouth, carrying the insect with it.

Insects found on plants are the favorite meal of frogs.

FOREFEET
have four fingers and are not as strong as the hind feet.

AT THE TOP
The white-lipped tree frog (Litoria infrafrenata) has a maximum length of 3.9 inches (10 cm) and is adapted for mountain climbing, jumping, and moving on flat areas. The pads on the tip of each finger and toe allow it to adhere to many surfaces.

The toe has a sticky mucous coating.

WHITE-LIPPED TREE FROG
Litoria infrafrenata

Spinal column
Its small number of vertebrae give it elasticity in the act of jumping.

9 VERTEBRAE
Aside from these, it has a urostyle—a cylindrical bone that results from the fusion of vertebrae.

Leg
Adapted for jumping and swimming

③ Fall
At this moment, when the frog extends its hind legs, it not only reduces air resistance but also helps with the entry into the water.

Fall
Each hind leg extends like an arrow.

THE JUMP
The toad's jump covers less distance because of its greater weight and because its legs are not as flexible as those of the frog.

17.5 feet
(5.35 m)

THE DISTANCE JUMPED BY AN AFRICAN FROG

DIVE
The body curves upward when it enters the water.

The hind legs boost the jump.

It closes its eyes for protection.

It lands with its forelimbs.

It rises in the air a few inches.

T REST   DRIVE   FULL JUMP   LANDING

Deep Embrace

R eproduction by amphibians is usually carried out in the water, where the female deposits the eggs, despite the fact that some species are able to deposit eggs on land. The most favorable time for this activity is during the spring, when the male sings to make his presence known. During mating, also called amplexus, the male positions himself on top and fertilizes the eggs as they come out. Then gelatinous layers absorb water and increase their volume, binding the eggs together in large masses. ●

A ROMANTIC SONG
The call that a male makes to mate with a female

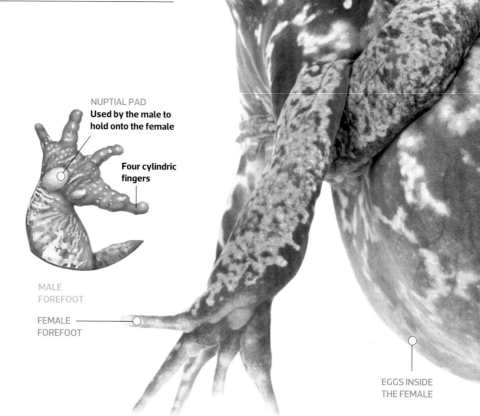

Amplexus

Fertilization for the majority of amphibians is external. In this hazardous process, the male, embracing the female in amplexus, discharges spermatozoa while the ovocytes are released. Both are released in great numbers in order to ensure the success of the process. This mating embrace can last from 23 to 45 minutes.

— 2.7 inches —
(7 cm)

Females are larger than males.

Weight
1.7–5 ounces
(50–100 g)

IBERIAN WATER FROG
Rana perezi

Diet	Carnivorous
Reproduction	Oviparous
Season	Spring

NUPTIAL PAD
Used by the male to hold onto the female

Four cylindric fingers

MALE FOREFOOT

FEMALE FOREFOOT

EGGS INSIDE THE FEMALE

SOME ANURANS CAN LAY UP TO

20,000 eggs.

LIFE CYCLE
The three stages of the life cycle are egg, larva, and adult. The embryos begin to develop within the eggs; then, after six or nine days, the eggs hatch, and tiny tadpoles with spherical heads, large tails, and gills emerge. Once the gills pass their function over to the lungs and the tail of the amphibian has shrunk and disappeared, the young frog enters the adult stage.

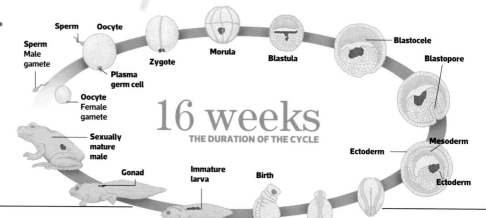

Sperm

Oocyte

Sperm
Male gamete

Zygote

Morula

Blastula

Blastocele

Blastopore

Plasma germ cell

Oocyte
Female gamete

16 weeks
THE DURATION OF THE CYCLE

Mesoderm

Ectoderm

Ectoderm

Sexually mature male

Gonad

Immature larva

Birth

Responsible Parents

Some males of frog and toad species play an important role in the protection of the eggs laid by the female. They pick up the eggs and help the mothers, and some even carry the eggs with them until the birth takes place.

EUROPEAN MIDWIFE TOAD
Alytes obstetricans
The male winds up the string of eggs that the female has laid over his hind legs. He carries the eggs for a month, provides them with a moist environment, and leaves them in the water so the young can swim away.

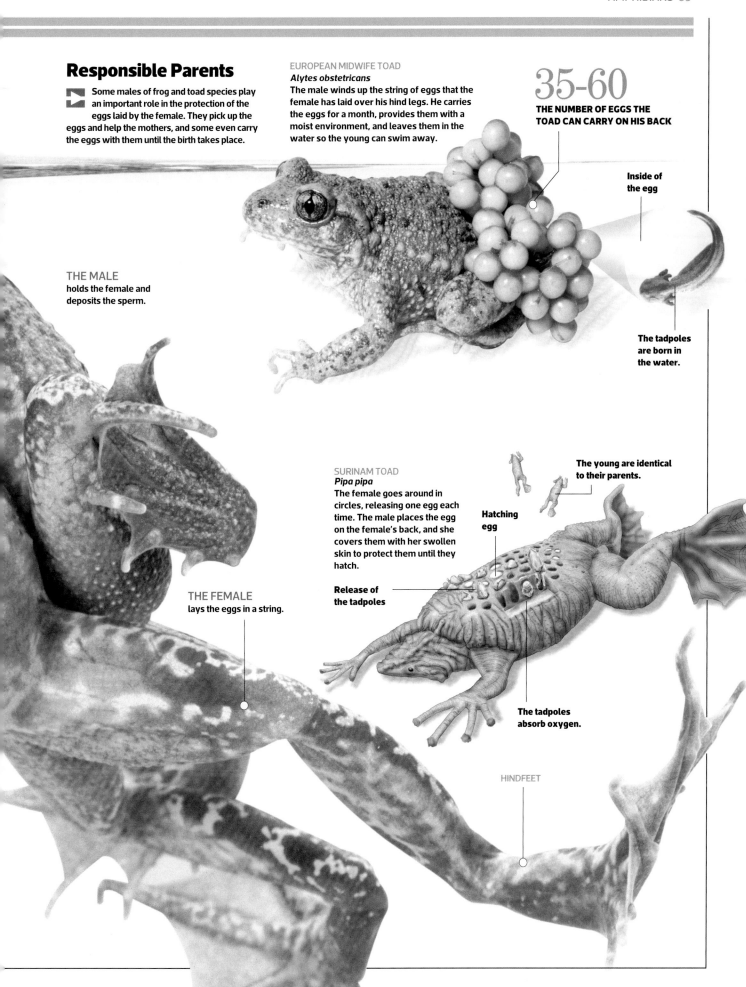

35-60
THE NUMBER OF EGGS THE TOAD CAN CARRY ON HIS BACK

Inside of the egg

The tadpoles are born in the water.

THE MALE
holds the female and deposits the sperm.

THE FEMALE
lays the eggs in a string.

SURINAM TOAD
Pipa pipa
The female goes around in circles, releasing one egg each time. The male places the egg on the female's back, and she covers them with her swollen skin to protect them until they hatch.

The young are identical to their parents.

Hatching egg

Release of the tadpoles

The tadpoles absorb oxygen.

HINDFEET

Metamorphosis

M etamorphosis is the process of transformation experienced by anurans (it can also be observed in amphibians from the order Urodela and caecilians) starting with the egg and ending at the adult stage. When they leave the egg, amphibians have a larval form. They then undergo very important changes in their anatomy, diet, and lifestyle, slowly mutating from their first stage, which is completely aquatic, until they transform into animals adapted to life on land. ●

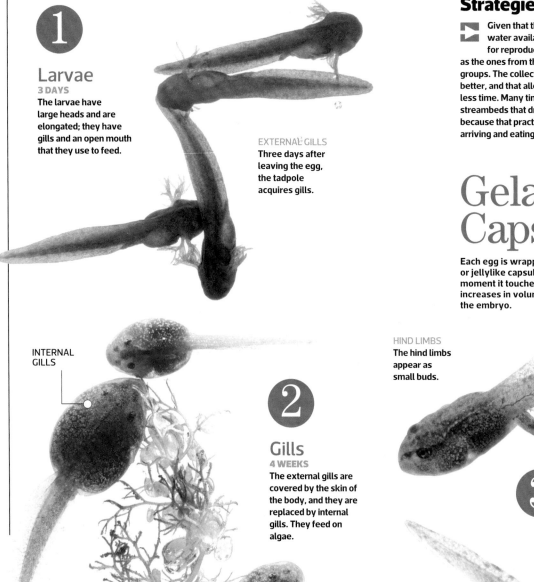

1 Larvae
3 DAYS
The larvae have large heads and are elongated; they have gills and an open mouth that they use to feed.

EXTERNAL GILLS
Three days after leaving the egg, the tadpole acquires gills.

INTERNAL GILLS

2 Gills
4 WEEKS
The external gills are covered by the skin of the body, and they are replaced by internal gills. They feed on algae.

Strategies

Given that there often are not enough bodies of water available (or not enough that are adequate for reproduction), many frogs and toads such as the ones from this species form large proliferation groups. The collective mass of eggs can retain heat better, and that allows the tadpoles to be hatched in less time. Many times frogs and toads use lakes and streambeds that dry out at certain times of the year, because that practice prevents other animals from arriving and eating the eggs and tadpoles.

Gelatinous Capsule

Each egg is wrapped in a gelatinous or jellylike capsule that expands the moment it touches the water and thus increases in volume to protect the embryo.

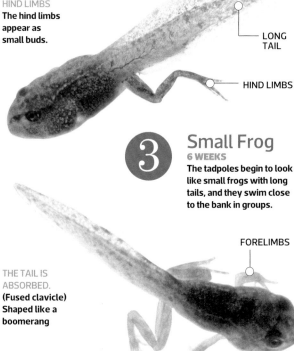

HIND LIMBS
The hind limbs appear as small buds.

LONG TAIL

HIND LIMBS

3 Small Frog
6 WEEKS
The tadpoles begin to look like small frogs with long tails, and they swim close to the bank in groups.

FORELIMBS

THE TAIL IS ABSORBED.
(Fused clavicle) Shaped like a boomerang

Cycle

METAMORPHOSIS
The development of the common European frog from egg to adult takes approximately 16 weeks.

Mother Frog and Her Eggs

Despite the fact that the survival instinct of anurans is not fully developed, frogs and toads somehow take care of their future young. Laying eggs in great quantities ensures that many tadpoles will be able to escape predators who feed on the eggs. The gelatinous layer also protects the eggs from other predators. Some frogs even care for their tadpoles by nestling them on their backs. An example of such a frog is the Surinam toad.

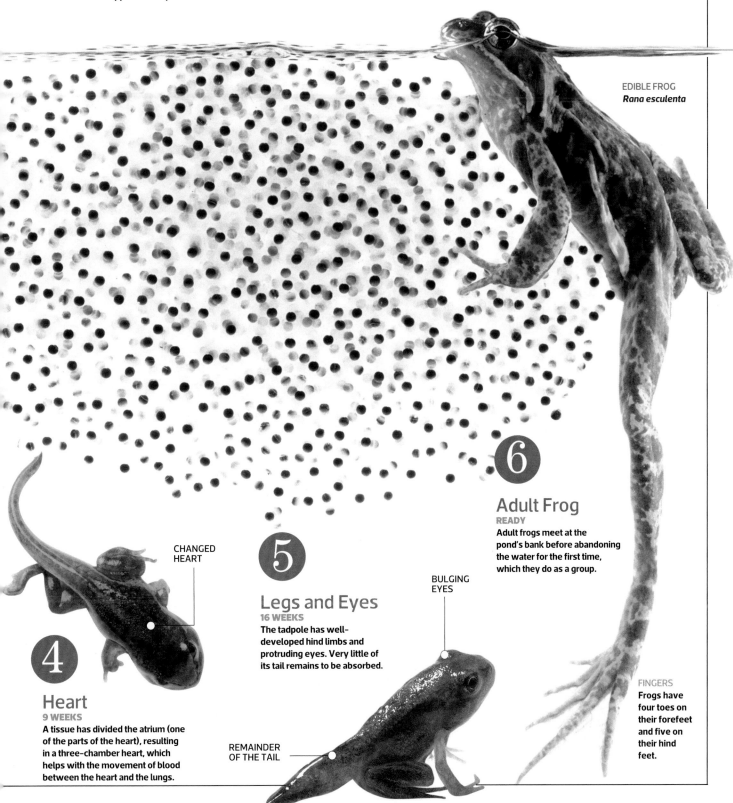

EDIBLE FROG
Rana esculenta

6

Adult Frog
READY
Adult frogs meet at the pond's bank before abandoning the water for the first time, which they do as a group.

BULGING EYES

5

Legs and Eyes
16 WEEKS
The tadpole has well-developed hind limbs and protruding eyes. Very little of its tail remains to be absorbed.

CHANGED HEART

4

Heart
9 WEEKS
A tissue has divided the atrium (one of the parts of the heart), resulting in a three-chamber heart, which helps with the movement of blood between the heart and the lungs.

REMAINDER OF THE TAIL

FINGERS
Frogs have four toes on their forefeet and five on their hind feet.

Poison in Color

Not all that glitters is gold, nor is it healthy. The skin of some amphibians has glands that secrete poison. Color is a warning sign, a way of keeping possible attackers away, and also a way to defend territory during mating season. The most dangerous frogs are the poison dart frogs from Central and South America and the mantella frogs of Madagascar. They are a small, very sociable species that live in small groups, are diurnal, and, in some cases, live in trees. ●

WARNING COLOR BANDS

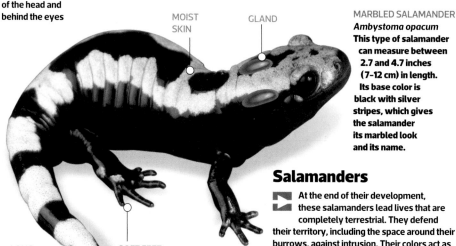

POISONED DARTS

The Chocó Indians of Colombia poison the tips of the darts of their blowpipes to hunt. They obtain the toxin by heating a live frog over a fire. In the case of *Phyllobates terribilis*, this yellow frog is so poisonous that rubbing the dart against the back of the frog is enough to make the dart poisonous.

NO TAIL

1 Tadpole. Has not yet developed the poison at this stage.

About

3,600

species of amphibians recorded in the world are poisonous.

2 Tadpole with legs. When the color is visible, the poison is deadly.

GLANDS

function the same as in frogs; they have glands that secrete poison on the skin and cover it.

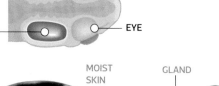

GLANDS
On both sides of the head and behind the eyes

EYE

STRONG HIND LEGS

3 Adult. The color is bright and distinct.

MOIST SKIN

GLAND

MARBLED SALAMANDER
Ambystoma opacum
This type of salamander can measure between 2.7 and 4.7 inches (7–12 cm) in length. Its base color is black with silver stripes, which gives the salamander its marbled look and its name.

TOXIC TADPOLES

Poison dart frogs, or poison arrow frogs, carry their tadpoles, sometimes one by one, to small isolated ponds (sometimes in tree hollows), where they raise them. There they develop both their color and the poisonous toxins that they secrete from their backs when they feel threatened.

LONG TAIL

SOFT FEET

Salamanders

At the end of their development, these salamanders lead lives that are completely terrestrial. They defend their territory, including the space around their burrows, against intrusion. Their colors act as a warning to would-be predators. Two rows of poisonous glands run the length of their bodies.

Frogs and Mantellas

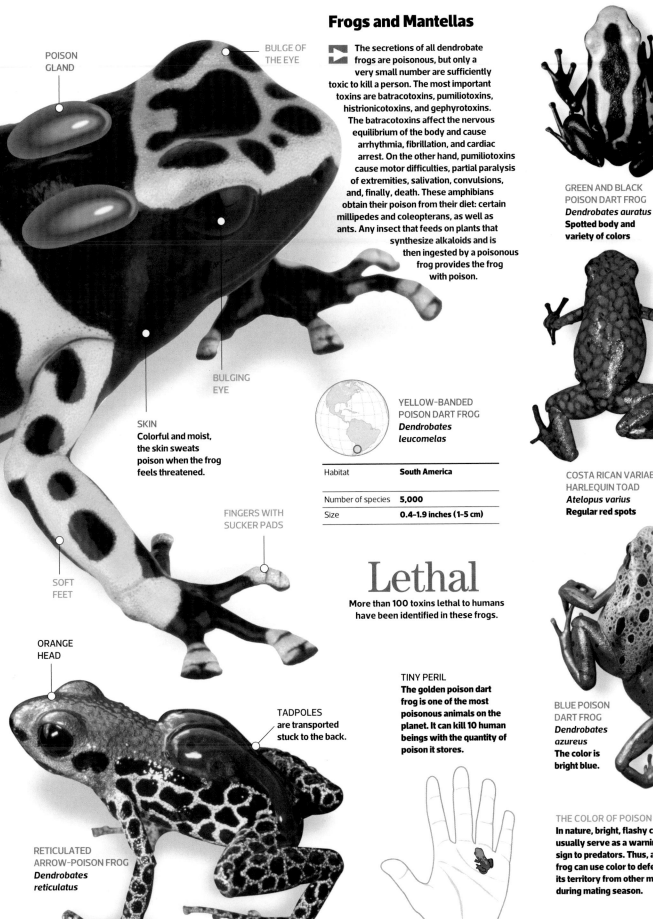

POISON
GLAND

BULGE OF
THE EYE

The secretions of all dendrobate frogs are poisonous, but only a very small number are sufficiently toxic to kill a person. The most important toxins are batracotoxins, pumiliotoxins, histrionicotoxins, and gephyrotoxins. The batracotoxins affect the nervous equilibrium of the body and cause arrhythmia, fibrillation, and cardiac arrest. On the other hand, pumiliotoxins cause motor difficulties, partial paralysis of extremities, salivation, convulsions, and, finally, death. These amphibians obtain their poison from their diet: certain millipedes and coleopterans, as well as ants. Any insect that feeds on plants that synthesize alkaloids and is then ingested by a poisonous frog provides the frog with poison.

GREEN AND BLACK
POISON DART FROG
Dendrobates auratus
**Spotted body and
variety of colors**

BULGING
EYE

SKIN
**Colorful and moist,
the skin sweats
poison when the frog
feels threatened.**

YELLOW-BANDED
POISON DART FROG
*Dendrobates
leucomelas*

Habitat	**South America**
Number of species	**5,000**
Size	**0.4–1.9 inches (1–5 cm)**

COSTA RICAN VARIABLE
HARLEQUIN TOAD
Atelopus varius
Regular red spots

FINGERS WITH
SUCKER PADS

Lethal

More than 100 toxins lethal to humans
have been identified in these frogs.

SOFT
FEET

BLUE POISON
DART FROG
*Dendrobates
azureus*
**The color is
bright blue.**

ORANGE
HEAD

TADPOLES
are transported
stuck to the back.

TINY PERIL
**The golden poison dart
frog is one of the most
poisonous animals on the
planet. It can kill 10 human
beings with the quantity of
poison it stores.**

RETICULATED
ARROW-POISON FROG
*Dendrobates
reticulatus*

THE COLOR OF POISON
**In nature, bright, flashy colors
usually serve as a warning
sign to predators. Thus, a
frog can use color to defend
its territory from other males
during mating season.**

Axolotl

his plump amphibian is a classic example of neoteny—the ability to reproduce without developing completely into an adult. The axolotl has a flat tail and large external gills, which most salamanders lose when they reach maturity and begin to live on land. The axolotl is mostly nocturnal and feeds chiefly on invertebrates. It, in turn, can wind up as the prey of a water bird. The axolotl was once considered a delicacy, but it is now legally protected.

AXOLOTL
Ambystoma mexicanum

Habitat	Mexico (Lake Xochimilco)
Habits	Mainly aquatic
Length	10–12 inches (25–30 cm)
Life span	25 years

12 inches
(30 cm)

Weight
1.5 pounds (0.7 kg)

LAKE XOCHIMILCO is the only place on the planet where the axolotl is found in the wild.

Lake Zumpango

Longitude 99°

Lake Xaltocan

Latitude 19° 30

Tenochtitlán

Lake Texcoco

Lake Xochimilco

Lake Chalco

Neoteny

One of this animal's notable traits is neoteny—that is, reaching sexual maturity while in a larval stage, never experiencing metamorphosis. Neoteny is caused by low levels or the complete absence of thyroxine as the result of a low-functioning thyroid gland. In axolotls, thyroxine can be generated under experimental conditions by administering iodine.

12 inches
(30 cm)

An adult axolotl can be 10 to 12 inches (25–30 cm) long.

Life Cycle

The female lays a large number of eggs. The time of incubation depends largely on the temperature. At 60° F (16° C), incubation averages 19 days. At the age of six months, the animals are very active swimmers. They reach sexual maturity at one year of age and adult size at between two and three years, never losing certain anatomical and physiological traits of the larval stage.

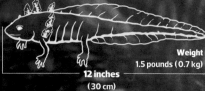

ADULT
At two or three years of age

EGGS

FULL-GROWN

LARVA

Regeneration

Another trait of the axolotl is its outstanding ability to regenerate its extremities and other parts of the body, including parts of its head. It can regenerate itself through the proliferation of stem cells in the affected area. These cells multiply and differentiate to replace the missing tissue. Interestingly, the ability to regenerate is shared by other amphibians of the order Urodela.

Mythology

In Aztec mythology, the axolotl (*atl* means "water" and *xolotl* means "monster") is the aquatic form of Xólotl, the god for which it is named. Xólotl feared death, refused to accept it, and sought to escape it using his powers of transformation. The legend recounts that, to flee Death, he ran to the water, where he became the fish called axolotl. This action becomes his final metamorphosis, because Death finally finds him and kills him.

EXTERNAL GILLS
are a trait that most salamanders lose when they reach maturity and begin to live on land.

COLORS
Usually they are dark brown with white spots. In captivity or in their natural environment, some are albinos with red or gray gills.

SKIN
Unlike salamanders and other metamorphosed amphibians, axolotls do not shed their skin.

EXTREMITIES
The extremities are fragile and delicate. In albinos, the bones can be seen through the thin, transparent skin. Axolotls have four toes on each front foot and five on each hind foot.

A Very Peculiar Tail

The salamander is an animal of the order Urodela that needs damp places to survive. It lives in a very limited range of areas, and it is highly sensitive to modifications in its natural habitat. Unlike frogs and toads, the salamander keeps its tail when it reaches adulthood. The tail makes up nearly half the length of its body. Salamanders, especially adults, are completely nocturnal. Their movements are slow when they walk or crawl along the ground. During the day they stay hidden under rocks, in underground burrows, and on tree trunks.●

COMMON
SALAMANDER
*Salamandra
salamandra*

Habitat	**Europe**
Order	**Urodela**
Family	**Salamandridae**

7-11 inches
(18-28 cm)

**Reproduction may
occur in spring,
depending on the
habitat and the
species.**

HUMIDITY
is necessary for
breathing through
the skin.

SKIN
On the back and sides, the
skin is smooth and shiny.
On the throat and belly,
the yellow spots are
duller and less numerous.

Anatomy

The head is narrow, with the mouth
and eyes smaller than those of frogs
and toads. However, in comparison
with frogs and toads, the salamander's
body is longer, but its feet are similar in
size and length. The salamander walks
slowly, never reaching great speeds,
and its limbs are at a right angle to
the body.

HEAD
Its head is smaller than
those of frogs and toads
because of the loss of
bony structures and the
presence of cartilage.

TAIL
The salamander has
a tail, unlike frogs
and toads, which
lose their tails on
reaching adulthood.

BODY
Long, with 16 to 22
thoracic vertebrae,
each one with a
pair of ribs.

FEET
Salamanders have four toes
on each foot. The salamander
pushes its body forward by
pressing against the ground.

EYE
Large and bulging,
with a dark-brown iris

Tongue pad

**The tongue
muscles retract.**

**Outer section of
the tongue**

**Retractor
muscles**

Feeding Habits

With its long tongue, the salamander can trap
its prey in a flash and quickly gulp it down.
These carnivorous animals use mainly sight and
smell to hunt. Because they are not very active,
salamanders need relatively small amounts of
food. If they obtain more food than necessary,
they store it as fat for lean times.

ITALIAN SALAMANDER

Life Cycle

There are three stages to the life cycle:
egg, larva, and adult. The eggs vary in size
depending on the species. Larvae have
feathery external gills. Metamorphosis
lasts until adulthood, when the salamander
loses its gills and switches to
breathing with lungs.

Defense

The Italian spectacled salamander has two
ways of avoiding its enemies. It plays dead, or
it curls its tail forward. Other species defend
themselves by using a toxic substance produced
by glands or by breaking off the tail, which
continues to move on its own and confuses
the predator.

1 EGG
Hatches into
a larva

55 years
LIFE SPAN OF SOME SPECIES

2 BIRTH
The larva is born with
feathery external
gills.

3 ADULT
Metamorphosis
is completed;
the salamander
reaches sexual
maturity.

CHANGE
The body grows longer;
the salamander begins
to breathe through the
skin and lungs.

LARVA
Metamorphosis
begins; the
salamander loses its
gills and switches to
breathing air.

LARGE ALPINE
SALAMANDER

Salamandra lanzai

is known for having
the longest gestational
period of all animals,
even longer than that
of elephants.

38
months
GESTATIONAL PERIOD

Newts

Along with salamanders, newts are the most primitive of terrestrial vertebrates. Of the three main surviving groups of primitive amphibians, newts most closely resemble the animals from which all amphibians are descended. Some of their habits are also more complex and varied. Most of the time they live on land, but during the mating season they return to the water. Unlike frogs and toads, newts and salamanders keep their tails as adults. They are found in temperate regions of the Northern Hemisphere.●

FRONT FEET
Newts have four toes on each of their front feet.

Courtship and Reproduction

Courtship and mating involve a showy exhibition by both male and female. The male must find a female of the same species and bring her a packet of sperm, which he deposits on the ground or in a pool. Fertilization is internal, and the female gathers the packet into her cloaca.

NEWTS

Habitat	Northern Hemisphere
Number of species	360
Order	Urodela

1 DANCE
Males are attracted by the female's belly, swollen with eggs. The males draw her attention with their showy pigmentation and the flexible crest along their back and tail.

2 EXHIBITION
The male swims in front of the female, displaying his nuptial attire. He raises the toothed crest on his back and slaps his tail while producing secretions from his cloacal glands.

3 CONNECTION
The male deposits his packet of sperm and then gently guides the female toward it, pushing her with his side. The female gathers the packet into her cloaca.

Newt Species

Amphibians are divided into three groups, distinguished by their tails and legs. Newts and salamanders have tails and belong to the order Urodela. Some produce toxic substances for defense from predators. They are very small; the largest newt may reach 6 inches (15 cm) in length.

GREAT CRESTED NEWT
Triturus cristatus
spends from three to five months of the year in the wat

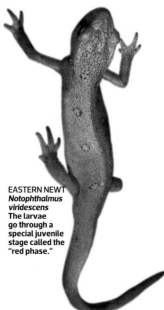

EASTERN NEWT
Notophthalmus viridescens
The larvae go through a special juvenile stage called the "red phase."

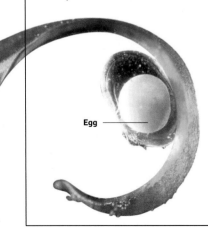

Egg

4 EGG LAYING
After the eggs are fertilized, the female finds a place to deposit them, attaching them to underwater vegetation or rocks.

Males have a crest, and females have only a yellow stripe along their backs.

DEFENSE
Some newts are highly dangerous because they release a toxic substance when attacked. One such species is the California newt. It can be recognized by its bright coloring, which serves as a warning to predators.

Anatomy of a Newt

Newts, unlike salamanders, have no grooves along their sides. Adults have elongated bodies 3–4 inches (8–10 cm) long, with well-developed tails. They have four limbs, with four toes on each front foot and four or five on each hind foot. Another peculiarity is that they have teeth in both upper and lower jaws. Their heads and eyes are relatively small. Smell is their most important sense for finding food and for social interaction.

PALMATE NEWT
TRITURUS HELVETICUS
3.5 inches (9 cm) long, with a pale belly

TAIL
Newts keep their tails as adults.

Feeding

Like salamanders, these tiny animals are usually active at night. The smallest newts feed on small invertebrates, whereas larger newts can eat fish, amphibians, and eggs.

HIND FEET
The hind feet are webbed in males but not in females.

BELLY
A white or pale belly is one of the distinctive traits of this species.

Male's crest

NEWTS AND WATER
As semiaquatic creatures, newts return to the water during mating season. They are found in North America, Europe, all of continental Asia, and Japan. Adapted to various habitats, they climb trees and dig in the ground in addition to living in the water.

MARBLED NEWT
Triturus marmoratus spends its whole life in the water, both as a juvenile and as an adult.

SMOOTH NEWT
Triturus vulgaris One of the most colorful

People, Fish, and Amphibians

The future of many fish and amphibians is uncertain because some species face fishing nets, loss of habitat, and the invasion of species cultivated by humans. In other areas acid rain is affecting the wildlife of lakes, rivers, and oceans. Fish in particular are very sensitive to chemical substances in the water. As for the world population of amphibians (more than 5,000 species of frogs,

SALMON FISHING
The salmon industry has
become a true economic and
social phenomenon.

toads, salamanders, and caecilians), one
third of all species are endangered. Even
though experts identify loss of habitat
as the main culprit, it is possible that
a little-known aggressor—a recently
identified illness caused by a
chytrid fungus—could be the
quickest killer of all. Many
similar facts and figures are
quite surprising. ●

Myth and Legend

Gods, demigods, princes in disguise, and religious symbols. In the field of myth, fish and amphibians embody powerful, mysterious forces of nature. Because they are aquatic, these smooth-skinned creatures are associated with "primordial waters." Thus, they symbolize the origin of life and resurrection. Through ancient texts, artifacts, and murals, we know that throughout history, many of these creatures have been regarded as supernatural and auspicious. ●

Trident
The symbol of sea gods. Poseidon could crumble cliffs or calm the ocean's water with one blow from his trident, as with a magic wand.

Christianity

The fish is one of the most important symbols used by early Christians. It may have been inspired by the miraculous multiplying of the loaves and fishes or by the meal shared by the seven disciples on the shores of the Sea of Galilee after the resurrection. But its popularity would seem to stem from the well-known acronym of five Greek letters that spell the Greek word for fish: *ichthys*. These words briefly and concisely describe Christ's character, as well as the Christians' beliefs about Him: Iesous Christos Theou Yios Soter–that is, Jesus Christ, Son of God, Savior.

It is believed that the early Christians traced two concave lines in the sand, which crossed to form a fish. The anchor, closer to a cross, was also used as a symbol.

FISH IN RELIEF
A mural featuring fish in bas-relief, a sample of symbolism from the early Christians

EARLY CHRISTIANITY
Basilica of Aquileia of a fish in one of its mosaic floors

The Americas

Challwa is the Quechua name for fish in Andean traditions. In the beginning there was not a single fish in the sea, because fish belonged exclusively to the goddess Hurpayhuachac, who raised them in a small well in her house. Once the god Cuniraya Viracocha, who was courting one of Hurpayhuachac's daughters, became angry with the goddess and threw her fish into the ocean. In that instant the oceans were populated, and humankind was now able to rely on this new source of food. A few fish keep sacred characteristics. An example is the golden croaker, which some peasants claim to have spotted at Lake Orovilca in Ica. In Central America, the Maya included the toad in the Popol Vuh, or Book of Creation. The axolotl takes its name from the god Xólotl ("monster" in Nahuatl), whose feet were backward.

XÓLOTL
Nahuatl name for the brother of Quetzalcóatl
The axolotl, *Ambystoma mexicanum,* is an amphibian native to Mexico that has divine origins, according to the ancient Maya.

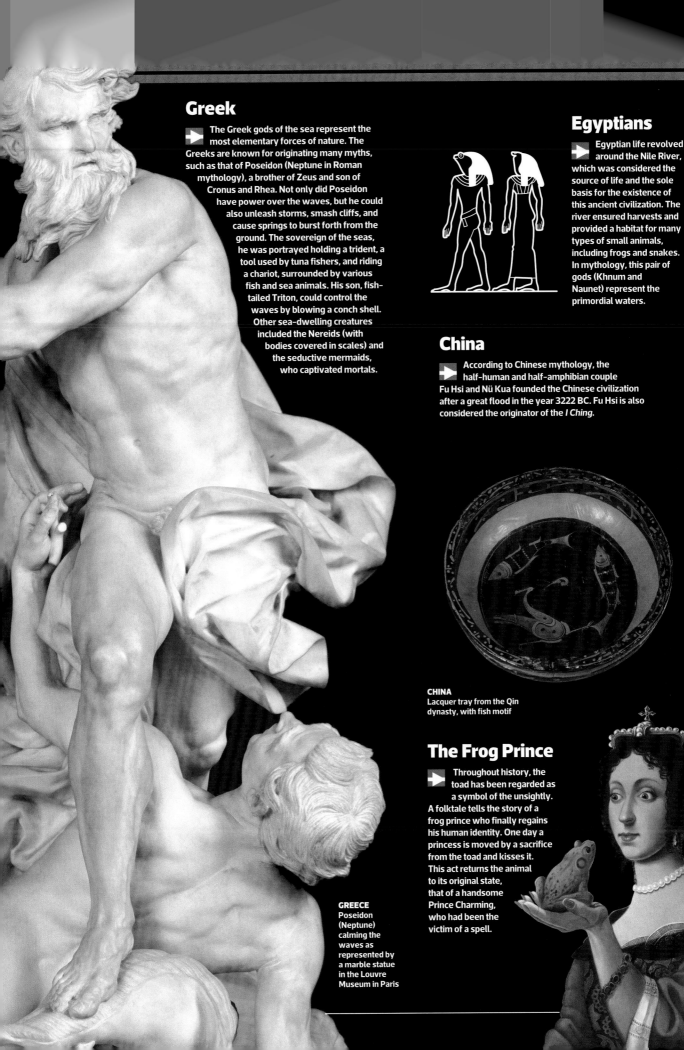

Greek

The Greek gods of the sea represent the most elementary forces of nature. The Greeks are known for originating many myths, such as that of Poseidon (Neptune in Roman mythology), a brother of Zeus and son of Cronus and Rhea. Not only did Poseidon have power over the waves, but he could also unleash storms, smash cliffs, and cause springs to burst forth from the ground. The sovereign of the seas, he was portrayed holding a trident, a tool used by tuna fishers, and riding a chariot, surrounded by various fish and sea animals. His son, fish-tailed Triton, could control the waves by blowing a conch shell. Other sea-dwelling creatures included the Nereids (with bodies covered in scales) and the seductive mermaids, who captivated mortals.

Egyptians

Egyptian life revolved around the Nile River, which was considered the source of life and the sole basis for the existence of this ancient civilization. The river ensured harvests and provided a habitat for many types of small animals, including frogs and snakes. In mythology, this pair of gods (Khnum and Naunet) represent the primordial waters.

China

According to Chinese mythology, the half-human and half-amphibian couple Fu Hsi and Nü Kua founded the Chinese civilization after a great flood in the year 3222 BC. Fu Hsi is also considered the originator of the *I Ching*.

CHINA
Lacquer tray from the Qin dynasty, with fish motif

The Frog Prince

Throughout history, the toad has been regarded as a symbol of the unsightly. A folktale tells the story of a frog prince who finally regains his human identity. One day a princess is moved by a sacrifice from the toad and kisses it. This act returns the animal to its original state, that of a handsome Prince Charming, who had been the victim of a spell.

GREECE
Poseidon (Neptune) calming the waves as represented by a marble statue in the Louvre Museum in Paris

Large-Scale Catch

The international demand for fish and shellfish has encouraged the use of highly efficient fishing vessels and techniques. The use of these vessels and techniques, however, has brought about increasing destruction of these resources and of the environment. Every year, fishing nets kill more than 300,000 whales, dolphins, and porpoises worldwide. The greatest threat facing many species is to become enmeshed in the nets. ●

Traditional Fishing

Traditional fishing is a widespread, small-scale activity practiced directly by fishermen using selective fishing techniques. Such harvesting of fish and shellfish is carried out with equipment such as harpoons, hand nets, fishing rods, and fish traps. The vessels may include anything from pirogues to small motorboats.

Local vessels
fish in surface waters. The fish they catch are usually sold in the surrounding area.

71.5 billion dollars
THE RECORD AMOUNT OF MONEY EARNED BY THE FISHING INDUSTRY

Algae supply
Collected as food or fertilizer, algae also provide the vegetable gelatin used to make ice cream and toothpaste.

Stone traps
strand schools of small fish when the tide goes out.

Raking cockles
Cockles and other shellfish can be gathered at low tide by raking the sand.

Net traps
are a series of cone-shaped nets with a cylinder at one end. They trap fish that swim with the current.

Commercial Species

Of the 20,000 known species of fish, only 300 are targeted for catching. Six of these represent half of the total catch.

HERRING

SARDINE

TUNA

MACKEREL

ANCHOVY

COD

33 feet (10 m)

Commercial Fishing

Commercial fishing fleets use advanced technology to detect schools of fish, and they use enormous nets of three types: mesh nets, dragnets, and sweep nets. Fish species that are not used for human consumption are also targeted commercially.

Purse seines, or surrounding nets

hang from floats and are dragged in a circle around a school of fish. Then they are closed at the bottom. These nets are ideal for catching surface species such as tuna and sardines.

1.24 miles (2 km)

Trawl nets

consist of a cone-shaped body closed by a sack in which the fish are gathered. These nets are maneuvered from one or two ships.

Overfishing

The fishing industry is an important source of food and employment around the world, and it provides the world's population with 16 percent of all animal protein consumed. However, environmental pollution, climate change, and irresponsible fishing practices are taking their toll on the planet's marine resources.

10% OF ALL SPECIES ARE EXTINCT OR RECOVERING.

Fishing boat with a purse seine

Trawl net

Trawler

Whaling ship

820 feet (250 m)

Long-line fishing

Many short lines with hooks hang from one main line. They are used to catch both surface and deepwater fish.

65 feet (20 m)

Gill net

HOLD area

Sonar waves are sent to the bottom.

The waves bounce back when they encounter schools of fish.

100 feet (30 m)

1,640 feet (500 m)

Sonar

is used to detect large schools of fish. Sonar waves are sent from the ship and bounce off the ocean floor. When they meet with a school of fish, they bounce back sooner.

Bag net

This net is used to catch lobsters, shellfish, and fish. The opening is designed so that the animal can enter the net easily but cannot get out.

Gill nets

hang below the sea surface like curtains, moving to the rhythm of the tides. Besides capturing fish, though, they attract and catch many sea mammals and aquatic birds, which then die.

Great Producers

Fishing is an important source of food and employment all over the world. These figures are in millions of dollars.

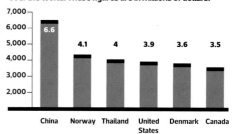

China	Norway	Thailand	United States	Denmark	Canada
6.6	4.1	4	3.9	3.6	3.5

Lures, Flies, and Bait

To spot, watch, cast the bait, and catch the fish. Humans and fish, face to face in hand-to-hand combat. Every fisherman or fisherwoman is a hunter, and knowledge of the prey is the basis of success. To catch fish, it is necessary to know their habits and preferences. Fishing methods, from fly-fishing to the use of cutting-edge technology, such as that used to catch tuna, depend on the area, the fish species, and available resources. Choosing the right morsel to tempt the fish (whether real or artificial bait) is another important decision. The key is to know which bait to use among the wide variety available and how to present it. ●

Where to Find Them

Knowing how fish breathe can be very useful for finding them. Arctic char, salmon, and most trout require well-oxygenated waters. They generally live in cold rivers at specific elevations, where the water is clear and clean.

Adipose fin, present only in the Salmonidae family

Fresh water

IS THE TYPE OF WATER WHERE MOST SPORTFISHING TAKES PLACE.

The tail has many spots, and they clearly differentiate the rainbow trout from the common trout.

Wild specimens are thinner than those in breeding farms.

2.7 inches (7 cm)

9.8 inches (25 cm)

Rainbow Trout
Oncorhynchus mykiss
The most popular species for sportfishing, this trout looks athletic and elegant, and it will attack anything that looks like food.

Fishing with a hook
This hook holds a piece of food that is tempting to the fish, so that when the fish bites, it will be hooked. Hooks are tied to a line connected to the fishing rod.

2 ACTION
The fish has seen the fly. The fish turns toward the fly, and when it takes the lure, the fishing line must be reeled in quickly.

Camouflaged jacket to avoid frightening the fish

Its tail is square-shaped and clearly forked.

Fins with white borders are characteristic of this species.

1 CASTING
Once the fish is targeted, it only takes one or two tries for the animal to become suspicious.

Waders allow the fisherman or fisherwoman to approach and make the crucial cast.

3 COMBAT
Once it has taken the lure, the trout begins to fight by diving and "sprinting" at high speed.

39 pounds (18 kg)

TROUT COME IN DIFFERENT SIZES, FROM 3.5 OUNCES (100 G) TO 39 POUNDS (18 KG).

They **hear** the lure.

SUCCESS DEPENDS ON BOTH THE LOOK AND THE SOUND OF THE LURE.

Rainbow trout can be recognized by the red spot on the operculum bone.

Fishing Strategies

Fishing with a fly, with a hook, with bait, and with lures. Every sportfishing species has its own challenges and thus demands distinct strategies.

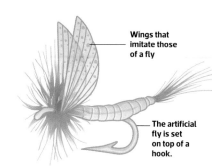

Wings that imitate those of a fly

The artificial fly is set on top of a hook.

Fly-fishing

is the most popular method among those fishing for rainbow trout. As the trout feed on surface insects, they are attracted by artificial flies that the fishermen cast.

Fishing with bait

These are natural baits placed on the hook for the fish to bite. The favorite baits for trout are fish eggs and worms, which are used with small sinkers tied to the fishing line.

Fishing with lures

Lures are objects used as bait to attract fish. They basically consist of a hook and some element that deceives the fish. They are used to capture Arctic char, anchovies, tiger shovelnose catfish, and trahiras.

Underwater, this fish can be identified by its white throat.

2.3 inches
(6 cm)

7.8 inches (20 cm)

Brook Trout

Salvelinus fontinalis
These fish are also known as speckled trout. When spawning season begins, they tend to form schools that travel as a group.

Fishing with floats

Fishing with floats and bottom fishing fall in the category of lure casting. This is a static type of fishing—that is, once the lure is cast, one waits for the fish to bite.

Endangered Species

ndiscriminate hunting, overfishing, and pollution of the oceans have pushed many species to the brink of extinction. Sharks and rays are among the first marine life-forms to be systematically studied, and 20 percent of their 547 species are in danger of disappearing. Slow-growing species are especially susceptible to excessive fishing.

Fish in Danger

➤ The situation is especially critical for angel sharks (*Squatina squatina*) and for the common, or blue, skate (*Dipturus batis*). The angel shark has now been declared extinct in the North Sea (after having been moved from "vulnerable" to "critically endangered" status), as has the common skate (which has been moved from "endangered" to "critically endangered"). The common skate is very scarce in the Irish Sea and in the southern part of the North Sea. As fishing operations have moved to deeper waters, the gulper shark (*Centrophorus granulosus*) has also suffered a substantial decline, and it is now in the "vulnerable" category.

HUMPHEAD WRASSE
Cheilinus undulatus

Status	Endangered
Cause	Pollution
Range	Pacific and Indian oceans

This fish lives in Indian Ocean coral reefs. A giant among reef fish, it can reach up to 7.5 feet (2.3 m) in length and can weigh as much as 420 pounds (190 kg). Its meat is prized for its flavor and texture. In many Eastern cultures, the humphead wrasse is considered highly valuable, and only the most privileged members of society can afford it.

HUMPHEAD WRASSE
Cheilinus undulatus

PERSIAN STURGEON
Acipenser persicus

Status	Endangered
Cause	Overfishing
Range	Caspian Sea

These fish swim upriver to spawn. Their eggs are highly desirable as caviar. This is one of five species of sturgeon caught wild in the Caspian Sea. It can reach a length of 26 feet (8 m) and can weigh as much as 1,760 pounds (800 kg).

ANGEL SHARK
Squatina squatina

Status	Critically endangered
Cause	Overfishing
Range	Mediterranean Sea and Black Sea

This shark was once a common predator in the North Atlantic, the Mediterranean, and the Black Sea. In the Black Sea, overfishing is especially excessive. In the last 50 years, the angel shark's population has declined dramatically; it has been declared extinct in the North Sea and has disappeared from many areas of the Mediterranean.

YELLOW-CROWNED BUTTERFLY FISH
Chaetodon flavocoronatus

Status	Vulnerable
Cause	Pollution
Range	Guam

It lives only in Guam, in the western Pacific, and only in coral reefs, especially black coral. From time to time this rare fish turns up on the aquarium market. In reality, little is known about the fish and its biology.

WHALE SHARK
Rhincodon typus

Status	Endangered
Cause	Indiscriminate fishing
Range	Warm seas

Although it is recognized as the largest fish in the world, little is known about the whale shark. It can grow to a length of nearly 60 feet (18 m), and it lives in warm seas all over the world. This fish takes some time to reproduce because females do not reach sexual maturity until they are 20 years of age.

COMMON SKATE
Dipturus batis

Status	Vulnerable
Cause	Overfishing
Range	Eastern Atlantic

This fish can reach a length of 8 feet (2.5 m). It has disappeared from many areas of Europe, where it was once common. It is still fished commercially, however. The common skate's large size makes it easy to catch in nets. It lives in the eastern Atlantic, the western Mediterranean, and the western Baltic Sea.

DWARF SEAHORSE
Seahorses eat mainly small crustaceans (copepods, amphipods, isopods, and ostracods), which it sucks into its tubular mouth.

PYGMY SEAHORSE
Hippocampus bargibanti

Status	Endangered
Cause	Pollution
Range	Caribbean Sea

Most seahorses are quite small, from the dwarf seahorse in the Gulf of Mexico, at 1 inch (2.5 cm), to the giant seahorse in the Pacific, at 13.7 inches (35 cm). In European waters, seahorses have an average length of 6 inches (15 cm). They use color as protection from the fish and fauna that share their habitat.

Dramatic Decline

Amphibians are considered by scientists to be the best natural indicators of an ecosystem's health. They are in a catastrophic decline: of all amphibian species, 7 percent are in critical condition, compared with 4 percent of mammals and 2 percent of birds. Of the 5,700 known species of amphibians, 168 have disappeared, and 1 species in 3 is in danger of suffering the same fate. Most of this decline—a phenomenon comparable in proportion to the disappearance of the dinosaurs—has taken place during the past 20 years. ●

Causes of Danger

The most important cause of the loss of species is the destruction of habitat through water and air pollution. Because most amphibians depend on fresh water to live, they suffer the effects of pollution before other forms of life. This makes them indicators of the condition of the environment. In America and Australia, scientists have identified a fungus that causes a disease called chytridiomycosis. This disease among frogs and toads has caused the amphibian population to decline by over 50 percent. This fungus advances 17.4 miles (28 km) per year and is lethal.

COSTA RICAN
VARIABLE
HARLEQUIN TOAD
Atelopus varius

Status	Critically endangered
Cause	Pollution
Range	Costa Rica, Panama, and Colombia

This critically endangered species is highly sought after for its bright colors, which have led to its illegal hunting. At the same time, the toad's habitat is being destroyed by deforestation.

SPOTTED
SALAMANDER
Ambystoma maculatum

Status	Endangered
Cause	Deforestation and pollution
Range	Eastern United States

Because of its forest habitat, urban growth and deforestation directly affect this salamander species, and so does environmental pollution. These are the factors that have brought about its endangered status.

CRAUGASTOR
TABASARAE
Craugastor tabasarae

Status	Critically endangered
Cause	Disease
Range	Panama

This fish is critically endangered because its population has declined approximately 80 percent over the past three generations. This reduction is attributed to the fungus *Batrachochytrium dendrobatidis*, and it appears to be irreversible.

GOLDEN
TOAD
Bufo periglenes

Status	Extinct
Cause	Pollution
Range	Costa Rica

The cause of the disappearance of this species is not yet known. There is speculation that the toad's extinction could have been caused by acid rain or by small variations in the environment.

COSTA RICAN VARIABLE
HARLEQUIN TOAD
Atelopus varius

7%
OF SPECIES ARE
ENDANGERED.

PERU
STUBFOOT
TOAD
*Atelopus
peruensis*

Status	Critically endangered
Cause	Infectious disease
Range	Peru

In the past 10 years, the population of this amphibian has declined by 80 percent. The species is now critically endangered. It seems that this animal is disappearing because of a fatal infectious disease that affects amphibians and that is caused by a fungus of the Chytridiomycota order.

KAISER'S
SPOTTED NEWT
*Neurergus
kaiseri*

Status	Critically endangered
Cause	Illegal trade
Range	Iran

This newt is endangered because the range of its habitat is less than 60 miles (100 km). The entire population of the species lives within an area of 4 square miles (10 sq km). Both the length and the quality of its life are declining, in addition to a decrease in the number of mature specimens because of the illegal pet trade.

MEXICAN
AXOLOTL
*Ambystoma
mexicanum*

Status	Endangered
Cause	Predation
Range	Mexico

The only natural habitat of the axolotl is Lake Xochimilco in the state of Puebla, Mexico, where it is very scarce. Foreign species such as koi and carassius, which were introduced by humans, prey on axolotl eggs.

DUNN ROCKET
FROG
*Colostethus
dunni*

Status	Endangered
Cause	Chytridiomycosis
Range	Venezuela

This frog is considered critically endangered because of a drastic, 80 percent decline in its population in the past 10 years. The devastation of the species is attributed to chytridiomycosis.

Glossary

Abyssal Fish

Rare species that inhabit depths of 8,200 feet (2,500 m) and below, where no light reaches. They have peculiar shapes, with large heads and strong teeth for eating other fish, because no vegetation grows at those depths. They attract prey with lure organs consisting of photophores that shine in the darkness.

Actinopterygii (Ray-Finned Fish)

Class of fish distinguished mainly by having a skeleton with bony spines in the fins. They have a cartilaginous skull and only one pair of gill openings covered by an operculum.

Adipose Fin

Small, fleshy lobe located behind the dorsal fin in certain groups of bony fish (for example, in Salmoniformes).

Amphibians

Animals with a double life. The young live in the water, and the adults live on land. Many need to stay near water or in damp places to avoid drying out. This is because some species breathe mainly through their skin, which can absorb air only when damp.

Ampullae of Lorenzini

Organs in sharks for detecting signals emitted by potential prey.

Anadromous Fish

Fish that reproduce in fresh water and live in the ocean as adults. Salmon are one example.

Anaerobic

Breathing process that does not require oxygen.

Anal Fin

Unpaired fin located in the middle ventral part of the fish above the anus.

Anguilliformes

Fish with a long, slender body without appendages, including eels and morays.

Aquaculture

The raising of aquatic organisms, including fish, shellfish, crustaceans, plants, and seaweed. These organisms are usually used as food for humans or animals.

Barbel

Fleshy filament that grows from the lower jaw of certain fish, such as sturgeon, catfish, and cod.

Bathypelagic

Fish that live at ocean depths below the mesopelagic zone, where light cannot penetrate.

Batrachians

Another name for amphibians. It comes from Batrachia, an old name for the class Amphibia. This nomenclature is considered out of date.

Benthic

Relating to the environment or habitat consisting of the ocean floor or of the organisms (benthos) that live buried in (endobenthic), on (epibenthic), or near the bottom.

Benthopelagic

Relating to organisms that are found either on the ocean floor or in open water. Usually refers to fish and crustaceans of deepwater environments.

Bioluminescence

Property of living beings that can produce light.

Bony Fish

Fish with bony skeletons and jaws. Their skeletons are relatively small but firm. They have flexible fins that allow precise control of their movements.

Bony Plates

Formations that grow from the skin and have a protective function for certain species. They usually cover the most sensitive parts of the fish, especially the head, although they can be found along the entire body, as in the case of the Placoderms.

Cartilaginous Fish

Fish with skeletons made of cartilage, such as the Elasmobranchii, a group that includes sharks and rays.

Caudal Fin

Unpaired fin at the lower end of the body, forming the tail fin in most fish.

Complete Metamorphosis

Phenomenon where the adult form of an animal looks nothing like the immature form; examples are frogs and toads.

Continental Shelf

Zone of the seafloor of variable dimensions, characterized by a slight slope and extending from the low tide mark to a depth of approximately 660 feet (200 m).

Ctenoid

Type of scale in which the free edge has spines.

Cycloid

Type of scale in which the free edge is rounded.

Diphycercal

Type of tail in which the spinal column extends to the ends of the tail, and the fin is symmetrical above and below.

Diversity

Degree to which the total number of individual organisms in an ecosystem is distributed among different species. Minimum diversity is reached when all the organisms belong to one species. Maximum diversity is reached in stable natural environments with a maximum variation in the substrate and environmental conditions.

Dorsal Fin

Unpaired fin located on the back, which keeps the fish in a stable position.

Eclosion

The moment when the embryo hatches from the egg.

Electric Organs

Organs of some species, such as electric rays and electric eels, specially adapted to discharge electric current.

Epipelagic

Relating to organisms that live in open water away from the ocean floor, from the surface to depths of approximately 660 feet (200 m).

Estuary

A coastal body of water, partly closed but open to the ocean, where fresh water and salt water mix.

Exothermic

An organism that cannot regulate or maintain its own body temperature is said to be exothermic. The organism's internal temperature depends on the temperature of its environment.

External Fertilization

Fertilization of eggs that takes place outside the female's body. The male releases sperm over the eggs after the female deposits them. The eggs are exposed to the outer environment.

Filterers

Fish that have evolved to take in water and use filters in their mouth or gills to extract from it only the nutrients they need.

Fishhook

Fishing implement, usually made of steel, consisting of a small bar bent in the form of a hook and tied to a fishing line. Fishhooks have different shapes depending on the type of fish they are designed to catch. The hook also carries bait to attract the prey.

Flatfish

Fish that have adopted a flat shape and live on the seafloor. They have both eyes on the same side of the head, a twisted mouth, and pectoral fins on top of the body. The "blind" side of the fish is in contact with the seafloor. Sole is one type of flatfish.

Flying Fish

Exocoètids, or flying fish, are a family of 70 species of ocean fish in nine genera. They are found in all the oceans, especially in warm subtropical and tropical waters. Their most notable characteristic is their unusually large pectoral fins, which enable them to glide through the air for short distances.

Fossil

Remains or impressions of former living beings that are preserved from past geological ages.

Fry

Newly hatched fish whose shape resembles that of adults of the same species.

Ganoid

Type of scale made of shiny, enamel-like material (ganoin) formed in successive layers over compact bone. The extinct fish Palaeospondylus had this type of scale. The only modern fish with ganoid scales are gar, bowfin, and reedfish.

Gill Arch

Bone that anchors the gill filaments or spines.

Gills

Organs that enable fish to breathe. They consist of filaments connected to the gill arches. The fish's blood is oxygenated in the gills and circulates to the rest of the body.

Gonophore

Anal fin transformed into a reproductive organ.

Grazers

Group of fish that nibble on undersea vegetation or coral.

Habitat

Living space in which a species finds the ecological conditions necessary for it to reside and reproduce.

Harpoon

Iron bar with an arrowhead at one end, often used to hunt sharks, whales, seabream, brown meagre, and other species.

Herbivore

Animal that feeds exclusively on plants.

Heterocercal

Type of tail fin in which the spine curves upward, forming an upper lobe of larger size.

Homocercal

Apparently symmetrical tail fin typical of teleost fish. It is not an extension of the spine.

Ichthyology

Branch of zoology concerned with the study of fish, including their anatomy, physiology, behavior, etc.

Industrial Fishing

Process for catching large quantities of fish from the sea for sale on the international or local market.

Internal Fertilization

Fertilization of cartilaginous fish, aided by the male's copulating organ. These organs, called claspers, developed from modifications of the pelvic fins.

Keel

Ridge or fleshy border along the sides of the caudal peduncle.

Larva

Immature but separate life-form, quite different from the adult.

Lateral Line

Line along the sides of the fish's body consisting of a series of pores.

Luminous Organs

Most fish in the ocean depths have bioluminescent organs that shine in the darkness and are used to attract prey or to communicate.

Lungfish

Fish that appeared in the Mesozoic Era, 250 million years ago. Like amphibians, these species breathe with lungs and are considered living fossils. Only three species have survived to the present.

Lure

Fixed or articulate lures are used in fishing to imitate small fish that are the prey of larger predatory fish.

Mesopelagic

Relating to organisms that live in the ocean depths, where light is dim. The mesopelagic zone is intermediate between the upper or euphotic (well-lit) zone and the lower or aphotic (lightless) zone.

Metamorphosis

Drastic change in the shape and behavior of an animal, usually during growth from an immature phase to maturity.

Migration

Travel (vertically in depth, horizontally toward the coast or along the coast) by schools of fish at more or less regular intervals (daily or seasonally), prompted by factors such as temperature, light, feeding, reproduction, etc.

Mimicry

Ability of certain organisms to modify their appearance to resemble elements of their habitat or other, better protected species, using camouflage to hide from their predators or prey.

Mouth Incubation

Mode of gestation for certain fish species that incubate the eggs inside their mouth and spit them into a burrow to feed. When the eggs hatch, the parent protects the young inside its mouth.

Multispecific Fishing

The harvesting of many species of fish and shellfish, with no particular species considered more important than the rest. This type of fishing is done in tropical and subtropical waters.

Oceanic

Region of open water beyond the edge of the continental shelf or island coasts.

Operculum

Gill cover of bony fish.

Osteichthyes

Class of fish that includes all bony fish, characterized by a highly ossified skeleton. This is contrasted with the class Chondrichthyes, including fish with cartilaginous skeletons (rays, skates, chimaeras, and sharks).

Ovoviviparous

Describing prenatal development of the young within the egg capsule, which is stored inside the female's body.

Parasite

Organism that feeds on organic substances of another living being or host, with which it lives in temporary or permanent contact, either within the host's body (endoparasite) or outside of the host's body (ectoparasite). Such an organism can cause sickness in the host.

Pectoral Fin

Paired fins located in the thoracic region, behind the gill openings.

Peduncle

Structure that acts as a support. In fish, it is a part of the fish's body located between the tail fin and the anal fin.

Pelagic

Relating to organisms that live at or near the ocean's surface.

Photophore

Mucous glands modified for the production of light. The light can come from symbiotic phosphorescent bacteria or from oxidation processes within the tissues.

Phytoplankton

Microscopic plants, of great importance as the basic link in most underwater food chains.

Placoid

Scales typical of cartilaginous fish and other ancient species. These scales are made of pulp, dentine, and enamel like that found in teeth, and they have a small protrusion. They are usually very small and point outward.

Plankton

Group of floating aquatic microorganisms, passively moved by winds, currents, and waves.

Port

Area along the coast, sheltered by natural or artificial means, where ships dock and carry on their operations.

Predator

Species that captures other species to feed on them.

Ray

In fish, bony structures that support the fins.

Reef

Hard bank that barely reaches above the ocean surface or that lies in very shallow waters. It can pose a danger for navigation. It can be inorganic in nature or result from the growth of coral.

Sarcopterygii

Another name for the Choanichthyes, a subclass of bony fish. Their fins are joined to the body by fleshy lobes, and those of the lungfish resemble filaments.

Scales

Small bony plates that grow from the skin and overlap each other.

School

Transient grouping of fish of the same population or species, brought together by similar behavior.

Shipyard

Place where small and large watercraft are built and repaired.

Simple Metamorphosis

Process in which the general appearance of an animal remains similar, although some organs atrophy and others develop.

Spawning

Action of producing or laying eggs.

Spines

Bony rays that support certain fins.

Spiracle

Gill openings between the jaw and hyoid arch. These are highly developed in fish of the class Chondryichthes and in a few groups of primitive fish. Their main function is to eliminate excess water optimizing water flow into the gill slits. Spiracles are especially important to rays when on the seafloor because the spiracle is where the water enters their gills.

Spoon

In fishing, a metallic lure trimmed with hooks. As the fisher reels in the line, the sinker bobs in the water like a dying fish to attract a larger fish and tempt it to bite the bait.

Sportfishing

Sport of catching fish by hand. In most cases the fish, once caught, is returned to the sea or river.

Stinger

Sharp point that grows from the skin. The order Rajiformes includes two families that have poisonous stingers on the final one third of their tail. The stinger is extremely sharp and has serrated edges.

Sucker

Structure formed from the pectoral and pelvic fins to generate pressure and stick to a surface. It can also be a modification of the anterior dorsal fin, the pelvic fin, or the buccal (mouth) disk of the cyclostomes.

Swim Bladder

A sac located in the anterior dorsal region of the intestine that contains gas. Its function is to enable the animal to maintain buoyancy. This structure evolved as a lung, and, in some fish, it retains its breathing function.

Symbiosis

Biological partnership established between two or more individuals (plants or animals) to obtain mutual benefits.

Tetrapod

Animal with two pairs of limbs, each of which ends in five fingers or toes.

Ventral Fin

Paired fins located on the abdomen.

Zooplankton

Microscopic larvae of crustaceans, fish, and other sea animals.

For More Information

National Geographic Society
Headquarters
1145 17th Street NW
Washington, DC 20036-4688
(202) 857-7000
Website: http://www.nationalgeographic.com
Facebook: @Natgeo
Instagram:@natgeo
Twitter: @NatGeo
National Geographic supports work in science and education, aiming to protect wildlife, oceans, and people's cultural heritage. Its website contains reference information about volcanoes and earthquakes throughout the world.

National Oceanic and Atmospheric Administration
1401 Constitution Avenue NW
Room 5128
Washington, DC 20230
(301) 713-1208
Website: http://www.noaa.gov
The National Oceanic and Atmospheric Administration provides information about opportunities to advance environmental literacy, including scholarships and internships for students.

National Wildlife Federation (NWF)
11100 Wildlife Center Drive
Reston, VA 20190-5362
(800) 822-9919
Website: http://www.nwf.org
The NWF seeks to protect and restore wildlife habitats and connect the next generation of Americans to nature.

The United States Fish and Wildlife Service (USFWS)
1849 C Street, NW
Washington, DC 20240
1-800-344-WILD
Website: https://www.fws.gov/
The USFWS protects fish and wildlife in the United States and enforces federal wildlife laws.

World Wildlife Fund (WWF)
1250 24th Street, NW
Washington, DC 20037
(202) 293-4800
Website: http://www.wwf.org
Facebook: @worldwildlifefund
Instagram and Twitter: @World_Wildlife
YouTube: World Wildlife Fund
WWF is known for its work in wildlife conservation and the protection of endangered species. Beyond animals, the organization also works to protect forests, freshwater, oceans, climate, and food.

For Further Reading

Bailey, Mary and Gina Sandford. *The Ultimate Encyclopedia of Aquarium Fish & Fish Care: A Definitive Guide To Identifying And Keeping Freshwater And Marine Fishes.* Southwater, 2015.

Hand, Carol. *Coral Reef Collapse* (Ecological Disasters). Mankato, MN: Essential Library, 2017.

Hastings, P., Harold Jack Walker Jr., and Grantly R. Galland. *Fishes: A Guide to Their Diversity.* University of California Press, 2015.

Herbert Howell, Catherine. *National Geographic Pocket Guide to Reptiles and Amphibians of North America.* National Geographic, 2015.

Hollar, Sherman, ed. *Protecting the Environment.* New York, NY: Britannica Educational Publishing and Rosen Educational Services, 2012.

Humann, Paul and Ned DeLoach. *Reef Fish Identification: Florida Caribbean Bahamas, 4th Edition.* New World Publications, 2014.

Stebbins, Robert C. and Samuel M. McGinnis. *Peterson Field Guide to Western Reptiles & Amphibians, Fourth Edition.* Houghton Mifflin Harcourt, 2018.

Index